THE
BAKING
BIBLE

Publications International, Ltd.

Favorite Brand Name Recipes at www.fbnr.com

All recipes and photographs that contain specific brand names are copyrighted by those companies and/or associations, unless otherwise specified. All photographs *except* those on pages 65, 83, 93, 107, 113, 131, 133, 247, 263, 273, 285, 291, 295 and 303 copyright © Publications International, Ltd.

DOLE® is a registered trademark of Dole Food Company, Inc.

™/© M&M's, M and the M&M's Characters are trademarks of Mars, Incorporated.
© Mars, Inc. 2005.

Carnation, Libby's, Nestlé and Toll House are registered trademarks of Nestlé.

Butter Flavor CRISCO® all-vegetable shortening and Butter Flavor CRISCO® No-Stick Cooking Spray are artificially flavored.

Some of the products listed in this publication may be in limited distribution.

Pictured on the front cover *(clockwise from top right):* Ultimate White & Dark Chocolate Chippers *(page 242),* Fruit Tart *(page 292)* and Berry-Cheese Braid *(page 80).*

Pictured on the back cover *(left to right):* Peanut Butter Chocolate Chip Loaf *(page 110)* and Nestlé® Toll House® Chocolate Chip Pie *(page 300).*

Illustrated by Julie Ecklund.

ISBN-13: 978-1-4127-2157-8
ISBN-10: 1-4127-2157-1

Library of Congress Control Number: 2004115114

Manufactured in China.

8 7 6 5 4 3 2 1

Microwave Cooking: Microwave ovens vary in wattage. Use the cooking times as guidelines and check for doneness before adding more time.

Preparation/Cooking Times: Preparation times are based on the approximate amount of time required to assemble the recipe before cooking, baking, chilling or serving. These times include preparation steps such as measuring, chopping and mixing. The fact that some preparations and cooking can be done simultaneously is taken into account. Preparation of optional ingredients and serving suggestions is not included.

contents

baking basics

Beautiful and delicious baked goods all have one thing in common—good baking basics. From ingredients to baking pans to garnishing, the information that follows is designed to help you get started.

ingredients

Keeping your pantry stocked with basic and frequently used ingredients is an important first step in baking. The following information will help you learn what ingredients you might need and any important details about purchasing them and storing them for maximum freshness.

Flour

Flours are categorized by the grain from which they come and, in the case of wheat flour, by the variety of the grain and the processing method used. Wheat flour is harvested from the tiny berries on wheat stalks. (Other grains, such as oats, rice, barley, rye and buckwheat, are also milled into flours, but these are low in gluten and must be combined with bread flour or all-purpose flour for the best baking results.) All wheat flours contain gluten, a protein that is activated when dough is mixed and is important in providing the structure in baked goods. Gluten amounts vary with the type of wheat: soft wheat has a low gluten content and is used in cake flour, while hard wheat has a high gluten content and is used for bread flour. Several types of wheat flour are typically available at the supermarket:

All-purpose flour is a blend of hard and soft wheats. It contains only the center of the wheat kernel, not the germ (the heart) nor the bran (the outer coating). Wheat flour naturally whitens through oxidation if allowed to age for a month or two, resulting in a slight cream color. Bleached all-purpose flour is whitened with hydrogen gas and benzoyl peroxide or other chemical agents; its color is pure white. Bleached and unbleached all-purpose flour can be used interchangeably. Most all-purpose flour comes presifted, eliminating the need to sift unless specified in a recipe.

Bread flour is ground entirely from high-gluten hard wheat. It is the preferred flour for yeast breads because it produces breads with the best taste, volume and texture. Some breads are made with all-purpose flour or a combination of bread and all-purpose flour. If you choose to substitute one flour for the other, be aware that the quantities used may differ slightly.

Cake flour is made from soft wheat flour and is used to produce delicate pastries and cakes. It is usually available in 2-pound boxes, sometimes in both plain and self-rising varieties. Be sure to purchase the plain cake flour, as the self-rising cake flour has leavening and salt added to it. If a recipe calls for cake flour and you don't have any on hand, you can substitute 1 cup all-purpose flour less 2 tablespoons for each cup of cake flour required.

Store all-purpose, bread and cake flour in airtight containers in a cool, dark place for up to six months. Temperatures above 70°F encourage bug infestations and mold, so if your kitchen is too warm, or for longer storage, refrigerate or freeze flour in moistureproof wrapping. Flour can also be stored in the freezer for up to one year. (Allow chilled flour to return to room temperature before using it.) It's best to transfer dry ingredients such as flour and sugar to airtight containers after opening them, because storing them in their original packaging can attract insects such as mealy bugs and ants. Always clean and thoroughly dry the storage container before adding new flour, and don't pour fresh flour on top of old flour.

Whole wheat flour is milled from the entire wheat kernel; it is coarser and denser than all-purpose flour with a greater gluten content and higher nutritional value. It is generally used in combination with bread or all-purpose flour to avoid overly dense or poorly risen loaves. (The bran in whole wheat flour interferes with gluten development.) Whole wheat flour is more perishable than other flours, so purchase it in small amounts and store it in the refrigerator for up to three months.

Cornmeal

Cornmeal is made from dried corn kernels. There are two grades of cornmeal: coarse, used for polenta and for cornmeal mush; and fine, ground from white, yellow or blue corn and used in baking, as a coating, and occasionally as a thickener. Fine grade cornmeal is more common than coarse grade. Either grade can be stone-ground, in which the whole corn kernels are ground between two enormous water-powered stones. This results in a meal that has more vitamins and nutrients than electric-milled commercial cornmeal; it is coarser in texture and more flavorful, but also more perishable—it should be stored in an airtight container in the refrigerator for up to three months or in the freezer for up to one year. Stone-ground cornmeal can usually be purchased from a natural foods store. Commercial steel-ground cornmeal, produced by a modern milling process that removes the husk and germ, is more finely textured and is the variety typically found in supermarkets. Store it in an airtight container in a cool, dry place for up to one year.

Cornstarch

Cornstarch is a smooth powder made from the endosperm (center) of dried corn kernels. It is used primarily as a thickener for sauces, custards and pie fillings. Cornstarch is available in boxes in the baking section of the supermarket, and it can last indefinitely when stored in a cool, dry place.

Oats

Oats are one of the most nutritious of grains, high in protein and fiber. Whole oats must be processed before they can be eaten—they are cleaned, toasted, hulled, steamed and finally flattened into flakes. Old-fashioned rolled oats are larger and coarser in texture than quick-cooking rolled oats; they don't absorb as much moisture so they produce slightly moister, chewier baked goods. Quick oats are essentially the same oats that have been rolled into thinner flakes, so they have a finer texture, cook faster and absorb moisture better. Old-fashioned and quick oats can

be used interchangeably in most recipes unless the recipe directs otherwise.

Oats are usually sold in cardboard containers in the cereal section of the supermarket; they should be stored airtight at room temperature for up to six months. Be careful not to confuse the different varieties of oats available: Instant oatmeal is not the same as quick-cooking oatmeal and should not be used for baking. Scotch oats, steel-cut oats and Irish oatmeal are oats that have been cut into pieces but not rolled. They are used to make cereal but are not good for baking because of their very coarse texture and the length of cooking time required.

Leaveners

Leaveners react with liquids to create air bubbles in dough, causing baked goods to puff up. Cakes and cookies usually call for one or two types of leaveners, baking soda and/or baking powder. They are not interchangeable, but both need to be somewhat fresh to be effective. Check the expiration date on the containers; the leavening power may be very limited or entirely gone if the product is older than the date on the label.

Baking powder is a leavener made of baking soda, cream of tartar and a small amount of cornstarch (to stabilize the mixture). When mixed with liquid ingredients, baking powder releases carbon dioxide gas bubbles that cause baked goods to rise. Almost all baking powder found in American markets is double acting—it releases some gas when it is first mixed with liquids, then releases the rest when heated in an oven. This double action means that batters and doughs can stand for a while before going into the oven without losing their leavening power.

To test if baking powder is still effective, stir 1 teaspoon into ½ cup hot water. If it fizzes, it's still good. If your baked goods turn out flat, however, it is not necessarily the fault of old baking powder—too much baking powder can actually cause baked goods to deflate rather than rise, and it will also leave them with a chalky taste. One teaspoon per cup of flour is the standard amount.

Baking soda, also called bicarbonate of soda, has four times the leavening power of baking powder; only a small amount is needed to make batters rise. (The standard amount is ¼ teaspoon per cup of flour.) Because baking soda is alkaline, it releases carbon dioxide bubbles when combined with an acidic ingredient such as buttermilk, brown sugar, molasses, honey, sour cream, fruit or chocolate. Baking soda should always be mixed with other dry ingredients first because it reacts immediately when wet; this is also why batters and doughs containing baking soda should be put in the oven as soon as possible after mixing—so the rising takes place in the oven rather than in the mixing bowl.

Baking soda is often added to recipes as a color enhancer rather than as a leavener. Since acidic doughs don't brown well, baking soda is added to neutralize their acidity and promote better browning.

Cream of tartar is a component of baking powder sometimes used with baking soda as a leavener. (It is actually an acid made from residue found inside wine tanks or casks after fermentation.) Cream of tartar is used most often to stabilize egg whites and achieve maximum volume while whipping them; it is also added to frosting and candy mixtures for a creamier texture. Cream of tartar is sold in small jars in the spice section of supermarkets; it keeps indefinitely if stored in a cool dry place.

Sugars and Other Sweeteners

All sweeteners are carbohydrates derived from the roots, stems or leaves of plants. Sweeteners do more than just add sweetness to baked goods—they improve tenderness, texture and color, and also help treats stay fresher longer. The most commonly used sweetener is sugar, most of it coming from sugar cane or sugar beets.

Brown sugar, a blend of granulated white sugar and molasses, has a soft, moist texture and distinctive flavor. It comes in two varieties, light and dark. Light brown sugar contains less molasses, has a lighter color and a more delicate flavor than dark brown sugar. Some brown sugar is not labeled light or dark—if the package only says "brown sugar," it is light brown. Both types add moisture, flavor and color to baked goods. They can be used interchangeably in most recipes but you may notice a difference in the results: baked goods made with dark brown sugar will have a stronger flavor and darker color than those made with light brown sugar.

Brown sugar dries out and hardens quickly when exposed to air, so the package should be sealed as tightly as possible after opening. Storing the package inside an airtight container and/or in the refrigerator also helps to keep brown sugar moist. The freshness of the brown sugar does affect the texture of the finished product—using hardened sugar produces a dough that is less creamy and baked goods that become dry when cool. If brown sugar does become too hard to measure, it can be softened in the microwave oven. Heat 1 cup at High power for 30 seconds, watching to make sure it doesn't begin to melt. Repeat the process if necessary.

Granulated white sugar is the most common variety of sugar. It is highly refined into tiny white grains, readily available in bags and boxes, and keeps indefinitely stored in an airtight container in a cool, dry place.

Powdered sugar, also called confectioners' sugar, is granulated sugar that has been ground into a powder and mixed with a small amount of cornstarch (1% to 3%) to prevent caking and keep it dry. The package may also include the words "10× sugar," which means that the sugar was processed to a fineness ten times that of granulated sugar—this is the finest powder and what is sold in supermarkets. Other grades of sugar exist, such as 4× and 6×, but they are only used by professional bakers and confectioners.

Powdered sugar dissolves easily and is most often used in frostings and glazes and to dust the tops of cakes and desserts; however, it is also used in some recipes to help create a very tender texture and tight crumb. As powdered sugar is less sweet and much lighter in texture than granulated sugar, the two are not interchangeable in recipes. Powdered sugar should always be sifted before using, since even a new package still tends to have clumps.

Corn syrup is a thick, sweet and highly refined liquid made by treating cornstarch with acids and enzymes that cause it to liquefy. It comes in light and dark varieties. Light corn syrup has been clarified; it is clear and almost flavorless. Dark corn syrup has caramel flavoring and color added; it has a stronger, molasses flavor. They can be used interchangeably unless a recipe directs otherwise.

Corn syrup adds moisture, aids in browning and helps keep baked goods fresher longer. It is also invaluable in making candy and frostings since it prevents sugar from crystallizing. (Sugar crystals make candy and frostings grainy and coarse.) Corn syrup is sold in glass and plastic jars and should be stored at room temperature.

Honey is a thick, sweet, golden liquid manufactured by honeybees from the nectar of flowering plants. (Liquid honey is actually extracted from the honeycomb by centrifugal force, then heated, strained, filtered and often pasteurized.) Its flavor and color vary depending on where the honey was produced and the type of flowers the bees fed on. The most common types of honey available in supermarkets come from the nectar of clover, orange blossom or lavender flowers, although a wide range of different flavors are increasingly available at gourmet stores and farmers' markets. Generally, the darker the color, the deeper the flavor.

Honey keeps indefinitely if stored in a sealed container in a cool, dark and dry place; however, it does darken with age and become a bit stronger in flavor. Honey may also develop sugar crystals but these do not indicate any deterioration of the honey. It can be easily liquified by placing the open container in a pan of hot water or microwaving the open container at High power for 20 to 60 seconds. (The water temperature should not exceed 160°F, as temperatures hotter than this will alter the flavor of the honey.) Honey adds flavor and moisture to baked goods and contributes to a softer, chewier texture. Honey also attracts moisture from the air, so treats made with honey may become even softer in storage.

Molasses is a thick, dark, strong-flavored liquid that is a by-product of the sugar refining process, obtained after the sugar cane juice has been boiled until it crystallizes to become table sugar. The remaining liquid is molasses. Molasses taken after the first boiling is called first strike, or light; it is the highest quality, sweetest and best for table use. The liquid may be boiled again to extract more sugar; the resulting molasses is called second strike, or dark, a good choice for baking. Light and dark molasses can be used interchangeably in recipes. Blackstrap molasses, the darkest and thickest, is taken after the third boiling. It has a bitter flavor and is generally not recommended for baking purposes. Sulfur is sometimes used in the processing of sugar cane juice, resulting in a darker molasses with a more pronounced flavor. Molasses should be refrigerated after opening.

Fats, Eggs and Dairy

Fat often plays an essential role in baking—it contributes flavor and moisture to baked goods and also helps maintain freshness. There are several different types of fat used in baking; each has different properties that affect the texture and flavor. For the best results, always use the type of fat specified in the recipe.

Butter, which is made from cream, is about 80 percent butterfat and 10 to 16 percent water. (The rest is milk solids.) Butter is scored by the United States Department of Agriculture (USDA) and assigned quality grades based on flavor, body, texture, color and salt. Grade AA (93 score) is the highest grade and the most common grade available in the retail market. Butter is usually sold in one-pound packages that contain four (4-ounce) sticks, both in unsalted and salted varieties. Unsalted butter is preferred by many bakers, as it has a fresher, sweeter flavor and less moisture, and it allows the baker to control the salt content of a recipe. Although it varies by manufacturer, salted butter has about 1½ teaspoons added salt per pound. Some experts recommend reducing the amount of salt in a recipe if you are using salted butter. Whipped butter should never be used for baking—it has too much air beaten into it and will not produce the same results. Similarly, reduced-calorie or reduced-fat butters should be avoided since they have a higher water content and will greatly affect the texture of the baked goods.

Butter should be stored in the refrigerator and used on or before the expiration date stamped on the package. Keep it tightly wrapped, covered and away from strong-flavored foods because it easily picks up other flavors and odors. Refrigerate butter for up to 10 days, or store it in the freezer for up to six months, with the original packaging wrapped in plastic wrap or placed in resealable plastic freezer bags.

Margarine is a solid fat made from hydrogenated vegetable oils (usually corn or soybean oil), along with skim-milk solids, emulsifiers, salt and preservatives. (The hydrogenating process means that pressurized hydrogen gas is forced through liquids to change them to solids.) By law, margarine must contain at least

80 percent fat; products with less than that amount are labeled spreads and are not recommended for baking because of their high water content.

Margarine is softer and more oily than butter and is available in similar one-pound packages that each contain four sticks. It should be stored in the refrigerator for up to one month or in the freezer for up to six months. Stick margarine, or stick butter-margarine blends (usually 60 percent margarine and 40 percent butter), can be substituted for butter in most recipes. However, the resulting flavor and texture of the baked goods may be different, especially in recipes where butter is the primary ingredient.

Shortening is 100 percent fat, made from soybean, corn, cottonseed, palm or peanut oil that is processed with heat and hydrogen. Available in cans and sticks, the original variety is pure white and flavorless, while butter-flavored shortening is yellow colored with artificial flavoring added. Because shortening does not contain water, it melts at a higher temperature than butter. Shortening can be used interchangeably with butter, but the flavor and texture of the baked goods may be very different.

Shortening remains solid at room temperature and can be kept, covered or wrapped, for up to one year. Storing shortening in the refrigerator will help it stay slightly fresher and whiter, but it is not necessary.

Vegetable oils, such as canola, corn, safflower or soybean oil, are 100 percent fat. They are used in baking to provide moisture and tenderness. For baking, make sure to choose a mild, neutral-flavored oil like those listed above. Peanut and olive oils have distinctive flavors that may not work well in baked goods. However, the flavor of olive oil is an essential part of many Mediterranean baked goods, so if a recipe calls for olive oil, do not substitute another vegetable oil in its place. Also, do not substitute vegetable oil for solid shortening, as the consistency of the dough or batter will be drastically affected. Store oils in a cool, dark place for three to six months. (Heat, light and time will turn oils rancid.)

Eggs are an essential ingredient in most baked goods. Egg yolks, high in fat, contribute richness, tenderness and color, while protein-packed egg whites add structure, stability and moisture. Eggs are sold by grade and size. The grade of an egg is not the measure of its freshness but is based on attributes, such as thickness of the white, firmness of the yolk and size of the interior air pocket. There are three grade classifications for eggs: AA, A and B. High-grade eggs (AA) have firm, compact, round yolks with thick whites—these are the best eggs for baking. The color of the egg shell (white or brown) is determined by the breed of the chicken and does not affect flavor, quality, nutrients or cooking characteristics of the egg.

There are six size classifications for eggs—jumbo, extra-large, large, medium, small and peewee—determined by the minimum weight allowed per dozen. Most recipes that call for eggs were developed using large eggs, so use large eggs when baking unless the recipe specifies otherwise.

Select clean, unbroken eggs from refrigerated cases and always purchase eggs as fresh as possible. The USDA requires that egg cartons display the packing date, which is indicated by a number representing the day of the year. For example, January 1 is day 1 and December 31 is day 365. An expiration date (month and day) may also be displayed. This is the last sale date and must not exceed 30 days after the packing date. Refrigerate eggs immediately after purchasing and store them in the coldest part of the refrigerator, in their original carton, with the pointed ends facing down. Don't store eggs in refrigerator egg bins or open containers, as eggshells are porous and can easily absorb odors and bacteria from other foods.

A very small percentage of American eggs are contaminated with salmonella, a bacteria that causes a type of food poisoning. It is important to handle eggs properly to avoid illness caused by this bacteria. Keep eggs refrigerated until shortly before using them. If a recipe calls for room temperature eggs, remove only the number of eggs needed and let them stand on the counter for no more than 30 minutes before using.

Do not eat raw eggs or foods containing raw eggs, which for bakers means you should not taste any dough or batter with eggs before it is baked. After handling raw eggs, wash your hands before touching other food or equipment, and keep your equipment and counter surfaces clean to avoid cross-contamination. If you have serious concerns about handling raw eggs, pasteurized eggs in the shell are now available in many supermarkets. The pasteurization process removes the risk of salmonella, while allowing eggs to taste and function like regular (unpasteurized) eggs. Because of this extra processing, pasteurized eggs are more expensive.

Egg substitutes are made almost entirely with egg whites (about 80 percent), plus artificial color and stabilizers. With no egg yolks, egg substitutes don't behave the same way as eggs do in baking—at the minimum, baked goods come out drier using egg substitutes, and there may be other differences as well.

Whole milk contains about 3½ percent milkfat, while **low-fat milk** varieties contain 2 percent or 1 percent. **Skim milk,** often called fat-free, has less than ½ percent milkfat. Unless specified, whole, 2 percent and 1 percent milks are interchangeable in recipes. Skim milk is too thin and will not produce good results.

Cream is the thick part of milk that contains a rich concentration of butterfat. Different types of cream are based on their percentage of butterfat. **Whipping cream,** also called **heavy cream,** has 35 to 40 percent butterfat or occasionally more. Almost all whipping cream is now ultrapasteurized, a process of heating that considerably extends its shelf life by killing bacteria and enzymes. **Light cream** contains about 20 percent fat, although the fat content can go as high as 30 percent. **Half-and-half,** made from equal parts cream and milk, has 10½ to 15 percent butterfat. Always use the type of cream specified in a recipe, otherwise the fat content of the baked good will change and the texture will be affected.

Flavorings

From spices and extracts to fruits, nuts and chocolate, there are numerous ingredients bakers should have on hand to create a wide range of flavors in baked goods.

Spices are the aromatic parts of plants, such as bark, berries, buds, flowers, fruit, roots or seeds. Unlike herbs, which are outdoor plants that can grow in many climates, spices come from plants that thrive in tropical regions. Spices should be stored in a cool, dry place in tightly covered lightproof containers. Do not keep them above the range, as heat and moisture will cause their flavor to deteriorate more quickly. Most spices are available ground or whole; ground spices should be purchased in small quantities since they lose their flavor and aroma very quickly.

Vanilla is the pod fruit of the tropical vanilla orchid, the only orchid that produces an edible fruit. The process to obtain vanilla beans is very time-consuming and labor intensive, which is the reason that pure vanilla has remained relatively expensive throughout history. The orchid flowers must be hand-pollinated, then mature pods are later hand-picked before beginning a tedious six-month curing process. Pure vanilla extract is made by steeping these cured vanilla beans in a solution of at least 35 percent alcohol, water and sugar, which acts as a preservative.

Imitation vanilla is made entirely of artificial flavorings, primarily by-products of the paper industry that are treated with chemicals to resemble the taste of pure vanilla extract. It can have a harsh quality that pure vanilla doesn't have, and it may leave a bitter aftertaste. Products labeled "vanilla flavoring" are a combination of pure and artificial vanilla extracts.

Like all extracts, vanilla is very concentrated and should be measured carefully. Vanilla extract should not be added to hot liquids, as some of the vanilla flavor will evaporate along with the alcohol. Vanilla extract will keep indefinitely when stored tightly capped in a cool, dark place. (If the cap is not sealed tightly, the extract will evaporate quickly due to the alcohol content.)

Other flavored extracts, such as almond, mint, lemon and orange, are concentrated flavorings derived from these foods by distillation or evaporation. Generally pure extracts are preferred over the synthetic versions in baking, but the imitation flavors can be used if necessary.

Dried fruit, such as coconut, cranberries, currants and raisins are often used in baking. They contribute flavor, moisture and texture to baked goods.

Coconut is the fruit of the coconut palm tree. The most common type of coconut used in baking is packaged sweetened coconut, available in bags or cans, flaked or sometimes shredded. Unsweetened coconut is sold in similar forms but can be somewhat harder to find; it is usually sold in health food stores. Be sure to use the type of coconut called for in the recipe. Unopened packages of coconut can

be stored at room temperature for up to six months. After opening, both types should be stored in a tightly sealed container in the refrigerator or freezer to retain freshness.

Dried *cranberries* are increasingly popular in recipes. Available in bags or in bulk, dried cranberries should be stored in an airtight container at room temperature for several months, or in the refrigerator for longer storage.

Currants are produced from drying tiny seedless Zante grapes. They are generally much smaller and drier than raisins, but the two are interchangeable in most recipes.

Raisins are simply dried grapes, usually Thompson seedless grapes. Like other dried fruit, raisins have a chewy texture and very sweet flavor due to their high natural concentration of sugar. Dark raisins are sun-dried for several weeks so they end up dark and shriveled, while golden raisins are dried with artificial heat and treated with sulphur dioxide, leaving them lighter-colored and plumper. Available in cardboard boxes or in bulk, raisins should be stored in an airtight container at room temperature for several months, or in the refrigerator for up to one year.

Nuts add flavor, texture and visual interest to baked goods. You'll get the freshest flavor if you purchase whole nuts and chop or grind them yourself, but many varieties of nuts are conveniently available in the form in which they will be used (chopped, ground or slivered). When buying nuts in bulk, taste a nut first to make sure that it's fresh—a rancid or stale flavor means the nuts are no longer good. When purchasing nuts in their shell, look for clean, unbroken shells without cracks or splits. Nuts should feel heavy for their size and appear well shaped. Shelled nuts should be plump, crisp and uniform in size and color.

Nuts are usually chopped or ground and sometimes toasted before being added to doughs and batters. A small quantity of nuts can be chopped with a chef's knife on a cutting board; for larger amounts it is easier to chop them with a food processor fitted with a steel blade. Use on and off pulses when chopping, being careful not to keep the machine running too long. (Most nuts have a high oil content and can easily turn to paste or nut butter when ground.) To reduce the risk of overprocessing, add a small amount of the flour or sugar from the recipe. Recipes usually call for either coarsely chopped nuts, which are pieces between ¼ and ½ inch in size, or finely chopped nuts, which are about ⅛-inch pieces.

Nuts should be stored in a cool, dark place until opened. After opening, store nuts in a tightly sealed container in the refrigerator for up to three months, or in the freezer for up to one year. (If you purchase nuts with no plans to use them right away, store them in the freezer.)

Seeds, like nuts, add flavor, texture and visual interest to baked goods. Because of their high oil content, they easily turn rancid and are best stored in an airtight container in the refrigerator for four to six months or in the freezer for up to one year.

Anise seeds come from a plant that is a member of the parsley family. The oval, greenish-brown seeds have a delicate, sweet licorice flavor similar to fennel. The seeds are a popular ingredient in many European and

Mexican confections, as well as in savory dishes in a variety of cuisines around the world. The seeds are available whole or ground. For the best flavor, purchase whole seeds and grind them just before using.

Caraway seeds are not actually seeds, but the dried fruit of a plant in the parsley family. It is these small, brown seeds, with a nutty, cumin-like flavor, that give rye bread its distinctive flavor. Caraway seeds are used extensively in Austrian, German, Scandinavian and Hungarian cuisine.

Poppy seeds are the very tiny bluish-grey to black ripe seeds of the opium poppy plant, which is native to the Mediterranean region. They add a nutty flavor and crunchy texture to baked goods, and they are frequently used in Middle Eastern, Indian and Central European cooking.

Sesame seeds are the seeds of a leafy green plant native to East Africa and Indonesia. These tiny oblong seeds are usually ivory colored, but brown, red and black sesame seeds are also available (for use in cooking rather than baking). Sesame seeds, regardless of color, have a slightly sweet, nutty flavor. They are widely available packaged in supermarkets

and are sold in bulk in specialty stores and ethnic markets.

Sunflower seeds come from the huge centers of the sunflower plant. The seeds are oval shaped with a hard black-and-white or grey-and-white striped shell. The shell is removed and only the kernel of the seed is eaten. The kernels, which are referred to as seeds, may be dried or roasted and salted and used like nuts in baked goods.

Chocolate comes from the cocoa bean, which is produced by cocoa trees in tropical climates near the equator, with most cocoa bean production centered in West Africa and South America. After the harvest, cocoa beans are fermented for several days, dried in the sun and then shipped to processing centers where

they are roasted. Roasted beans are cracked open to separate the shells from the kernels, or "nibs." Nibs are over 50 percent cocoa butter (a natural vegetable fat) that melts when the nibs are ground and produces a thick, dark brown liquid called chocolate liquor. At this point the chocolate liquor may be pressed, extracting much of the cocoa butter, to form dry, hard cakes which are ground into cocoa powder. Or, the chocolate liquor may undergo certain blending and refining processes, during which such ingredients as sugar, cocoa butter and condensed milk may be added to make different types of chocolate.

Chocolate should be stored tightly wrapped in foil or brown paper in a cool, dry, dark place, between 60° and 70°F. If stored at room temperature, the cocoa butter melts, rises to the surface and resolidifies. This causes the chocolate to develop a "bloom," or a pale gray film, which appears on the surface. If stored in a damp place, the chocolate can form tiny gray sugar crystals on top. These conditions only affect the appearance of the chocolate—not the flavor. The rich brown color will return when the chocolate is melted. Ideally chocolate should not be kept in the refrigerator (because chocolate will pick up moisture there), but this may be unavoidable if your kitchen is usually warm and humid. Stored properly, bittersweet and semisweet chocolate will last for several years. Because they contain milk solids, white chocolate and milk chocolate have a much shorter shelf life and should be used within about nine months.

Unsweetened chocolate, also called bitter or baking chocolate, is pure chocolate with no sugar or flavorings added. It is used only in baking and is commonly packaged in individually wrapped one-ounce squares.

Bittersweet chocolate is pure chocolate with some sugar added. It is available in specialty food shops and some supermarkets, packaged in chips, bars or one-ounce squares. If unavailable, substitute half unsweetened chocolate and half semisweet chocolate.

Semisweet chocolate is pure chocolate that is combined with extra cocoa butter and sugar. It is sold in a variety of forms, including one-ounce squares, bars, chips and chunks. It is interchangeable with bittersweet chocolate in most recipes.

Milk chocolate is pure chocolate with sugar, extra cocoa butter and milk solids added. With a milder flavor than other chocolate, it is widely used for candy bars and is also available in various shapes including chips and stars. Milk chocolate cannot be used interchangeably with other chocolates because the presence of milk changes its melting and cooking characteristics.

White chocolate is not considered real chocolate since it contains no chocolate liquor—it is a combination of cocoa butter, sugar, milk solids, vanilla and emulsifiers. White chocolate is available in bars, blocks, chips and chunks. Some products labeled "white chocolate" do not contain cocoa butter but are simply coatings, so check the ingredient list carefully for cocoa butter to make sure you have the real thing.

Unsweetened cocoa powder is formed by extracting most of the cocoa butter from pure chocolate and grinding the remaining chocolate solids into a powder. When cocoa powder is further treated with alkali to help neutralize cocoa's natural acidity, it produces a dark, mellow-flavored powder called *Dutch-processed cocoa powder* that is preferred by many baking professionals. The two types of cocoa are often interchangeable in recipes, but there will be some differences in color and flavor—baked goods made with Dutch-processed cocoa will be somewhat milder in flavor and darker in color. Unsweetened cocoa powder can be stored in a tightly closed container in a cool, dark place for up to two years.

bakers' substitutions

For the best results, always use the exact ingredients listed in a recipe. But if you have to substitute, try the following suggestions.

If you don't have:	Use:
1 cup cake flour	1 cup minus 2 tablespoons all-purpose flour
1 cup firmly packed brown sugar	1 cup granulated sugar mixed with 2 tablespoons molasses
1 teaspoon baking powder	¼ teaspoon baking soda plus ½ teaspoon cream of tartar
1 cup whole milk	1 cup skim milk plus 2 tablespoons melted butter
1 cup buttermilk	1 tablespoon lemon juice or vinegar plus milk to equal 1 cup (Stir; let mixture stand 5 minutes.)
1 cup sour cream	1 cup plain yogurt
1 cup honey	1¼ cups granulated sugar plus ¼ cup water
1 cup molasses	1 cup dark corn syrup or honey
½ cup corn syrup	½ cup granulated sugar plus 2 tablespoons liquid
½ cup raisins	½ cup currants, dried cranberries, chopped dates or chopped prunes
1 ounce (1 square) unsweetened chocolate	3 tablespoons unsweetened cocoa powder plus 1 tablespoon shortening
1 ounce (1 square) semisweet chocolate	1 ounce unsweetened chocolate plus 1 tablespoon sugar
1 cup semisweet chocolate chips	6 ounces semisweet baking chocolate, chopped
1 teaspoon fresh grated lemon peel	½ teaspoon dried lemon peel
1 teaspoon pumpkin pie spice	Combine ½ teaspoon ground cinnamon, ¼ teaspoon ground ginger, ⅛ teaspoon ground allspice and ⅛ teaspoon ground nutmeg

equipment

As with many activities, having the right equipment can bridge the distance between failure and success in baking. When choosing baking utensils, make sure that you purchase the best quality that you can afford—these items may cost a little more, but they are worth the investment since they will produce better results and last longer.

Measuring Cups

All bakers need two types of measuring cups. Dry measuring cups are used for ingredients such as sugar and flour, as well as for solid shortening. They come in sets of nested and graduated cups made of metal or plastic, including ¼ cup, ⅓ cup, ½ cup and 1 cup measures. (Some sets may also include ⅛ cup, ⅔ cup and ¾ cup as well.) Dry measuring cups do not measure liquids accurately.

Liquid measuring cups are, as the name implies, just for measuring liquids. They are available in glass, plastic and metal, but clear glass is the most practical choice—you can see the liquid you are measuring and it is a heatproof material. Liquid measuring cups have calibrations marked on the side, a small pouring spout and a handle opposite the spout; they come in 1-cup, 2-cup and 4-cup sizes.

Measuring Spoons

Measuring spoons come in nested sets of ¼ teaspoon, ½ teaspoon, 1 teaspoon and 1 tablespoon. (Some sets also include ⅛ teaspoon and 1½ teaspoons.) Available in metal or plastic, measuring spoons are used to measure small amounts of either dry or liquid ingredients. Do not substitute the teaspoons and tablespoons from your everyday flatware to measure ingredients; these spoons don't hold the same amount as measuring spoons.

Spatulas

Rubber spatulas, sometimes called scrapers, are flexible utensils with a paddlelike rubber, plastic or nylon head attached to a handle. They come in a wide variety of sizes and are ideal for scraping out the insides of bowls, containers and measuring cups. The larger ones are also good for blending dough and folding delicate mixtures together. Some of the newer rubber spatulas are heatproof; however, they are not as flexible as regular rubber spatulas.

Wide flexible metal spatulas, also called pancake turners, are a necessity for removing baked cookies from baking sheets. These spatulas have a flat, square or rectangular metal blade attached to a plastic or wooden handle. The spatula blade should be wide enough to slide under and pick up a whole cookie without having the cookie hang over the edges of the blade. The thinner the metal, the easier it is to slide under cookies without breaking or mangling them.

Long narrow metal spatulas have thin metal blades attached to plastic or wooden handles. They are useful for leveling off dry ingredients when measuring, loosening a baked and cooled cake from its pan, and are ideal for spreading batters and frostings. Some are 8 inches long and rigid whereas others are shorter and flexible. A flat spatula forms a straight line from handle to blade. An offset spatula is angled near the handle, causing the handle to be raised slightly.

Wire Whisks

Made of stainless steel wires that loop to form a bulbous shape, wire whisks are designed to aerate and mix. Larger balloon-type whisks are used for whipping air into ingredients such as egg whites and cream, while small and medium whisks are used for stirring hot mixtures as they cook and blending ingredients together without beating a lot of air into the mixture. When purchasing whisks, choose those that have sturdy wires and handles that are easy to grip.

Knives

Good-quality knives are important in baking as well as cooking, but only a few of them are used with regularity. A chef's knife has a wide, slightly curved blade from 7 to 12 inches long; it is used for most chopping tasks (such as nuts, dried fruit or chocolate) and for slicing rolls of dough. A paring knife has a short 2- to 3-inch-long blade and is used for peeling and slicing fruit, cutting out garnishes and other small jobs. A long serrated knife is useful for cutting bread.

Sifter

A flour sifter consists of a fine mesh screen and a mechanism to push flour through the mesh. Sifting aerates dry ingredients such as flour, powdered sugar and cocoa powder; it also breaks up lumps and gives dry mixtures a uniform consistency. A sifter with a 2- to 3-cup capacity and a crank-type handle is a good choice, but a strainer can be used instead if you don't have a sifter. Never wash a sifter; just wipe it out with a damp paper towel.

Graters

A four-sided box grater is a versatile and inexpensive tool with several different size openings; it can be used for grating citrus peel and chocolate in addition to its more common functions, grating cheese and vegetables. Smaller graters with handles may be easier to use and more convenient for baking jobs—these can be kept in a drawer or hung on a hook with other utensils.

Double Boiler

A double boiler consists of two stacked pans. The top pan, which holds food, nestles in the bottom pan, which holds an inch or two of simmering water. (The bottom of the top pan should never touch the water—it should only be warmed by the steam.) The purpose of a double boiler is to protect heat-sensitive foods like chocolate from direct heat. You can make your own double boiler by setting a stainless steel bowl over a pot of simmering water.

Rolling Pin

Rolling pins are used to roll out dough for pies and cutout cookies. They can be made from hardwood or marble or sometimes from metal or plastic. The typical American rolling pin is made of wood, has a handle on each end and rolls on bearings. The French version has no handles. A heavy rolling pin allows for the most efficient rolling, because the weight of the pin does most of the work, requiring less effort from the user. Wood rolling pins should be wiped clean with a dry cloth (rather than washed) to prevent warping.

Pastry Blender

This hand-held tool consists of several U-shaped wires or metal blades attached to a handle. It is used to cut butter or shortening into flour, which is an essential step in making pie dough. Two knives can also be used if you don't have a pastry blender on hand.

Pastry Brushes

Pastry brushes are small, flat brushes made of natural bristles, such as boar bristles, or nylon. They are primarily used to apply melted butter or glazes to baked goods before or after baking, but they are also useful for brushing off excess flour from doughs and even for buttering the insides of baking pans. Brushes should be washed by hand with hot, soapy water, rinsed well, then air dried after reshaping the bristles. Nylon bristles tend to tear dough and may begin to melt when they come in contact with heat; boar bristle brushes are more expensive but last longer.

Pastry Bag

A pastry bag, also called a decorating bag, is a cone-shaped bag made of canvas, plastic or plastic-lined cloth. It is used to pipe foods, such as frosting, whipped cream, or dough in a decorative pattern. It is open at both ends. The food to be piped is placed

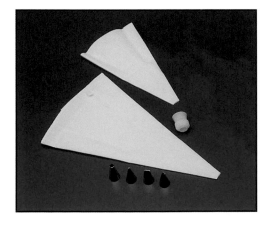

in the larger opening, while the smaller opening is fitted with decorative tips made of plastic or metal. (A small, resealable plastic food storage bag with a tiny hole cut from the corner of the bag can also take the place of a pastry bag for simple decorating.) A quick alternative to a pastry bag for decorating baked goods is a plastic squeeze bottle—filled with melted chocolate or icing, it can make drizzling and decorating easier, especially for the novice.

Parchment Paper

Parchment is heavy paper that is impervious to grease and moisture. It is sold in sheets and rolls at gourmet kitchenware stores and at many supermarkets. When used to line baking sheets and pans, parchment paper provides a nonstick surface and allows for effortless removal of baked goods (and makes cleanup very easy). Parchment paper can also be made into cones that function as disposable pastry bags to pipe icing or chocolate.

Oven Thermometer

Actual oven temperatures frequently vary quite a bit from the dial setting, so it is essential to keep a good-quality mercury oven thermometer in your oven all the time and adjust the dial setting to compensate as necessary. Most home ovens are off between 5 and 50 degrees, and sometimes even more. If your oven temperature isn't correct, your baked goods will be underbaked or overbaked.

Baking Pans

A **baking pan** is made of metal and has a square or rectangular shape with straight sides at least 1½ inches high. The most common sizes are 8 and 9 inches square; 11×7×2 inches; and 13×9×2 inches. Baking pans are designed for cakes and bar cookies. Shiny aluminum pans are ideal for producing a tender, lightly browned cake crust. Baking pans with dark finishes will absorb heat more quickly than shiny baking pans. When using baking pans with dark finishes or when substituting glass bakeware in recipes that call for baking pans, reduce the oven temperature by 25°F.

A **baking sheet** (often referred to as a cookie sheet) is a flat,

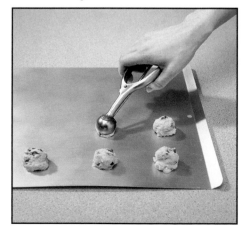

rigid sheet of metal on which stiff dough is baked into cookies, rolls, biscuits, etc. It has a low lip on one or more sides for ease in handling; a lip higher than ½ inch interferes with surface browning, especially of cookies. The type of surface also determines the browning characteristics of the baking sheet. Shiny finishes promote even browning. Dark metal baking sheets absorb more heat and cause food to brown quickly. Insulated baking sheets have a layer of air sandwiched between two sheets of aluminum which helps to prevent excess browning but increases baking time. (Some cookie doughs may also spread more on these sheets.) Nonstick finishes minimize sticking and make cleanup easier. Baking sheets vary in size. Before buying, know the dimensions of your oven. A baking sheet should fit on an oven rack with at least one inch of space on all sides between the edge of the sheet and the oven wall. Otherwise, heat circulation will be hampered.

A **bundt pan** is a fluted tube pan traditionally used to bake a densely textured bundt cake. Bundt pans usually measure 10 inches in diameter with a 12-cup capacity. They are traditionally made of cast aluminum with a nonstick interior coating but are also available in lightweight aluminum. Generously greasing the fluted sides and center tube is extremely important to prevent sticking. **Mini bundt pans** are also available in several sizes (½-cup, ¾-cup, 1-cup, etc.) and shapes (straight, fluted, flowers, etc.). To make sure that the pan you are using is the size called for in the recipe, measure the amount of water that one bundt form will hold.

A **cake pan,** or layer pan, is a round baking pan with a straight side at least 1½ inches high. Pans made of aluminum or heavy-gauge steel will produce a cake with a delicate, tender crust. Besides the most common round 8- or 9-inch cake pans, there is a wide array of pans available that measure from 3 to 24 inches in diameter. Cake pans also come in a variety of specialty shapes.

A **jelly-roll pan** is a rectangular baking pan with 1-inch-high sides. It is used to make a thin sponge cake that can be spread with jelly, and rolled into a jelly roll. Jelly-roll pans are also used for making thin sheet cakes or bar cookies. Standard pans measure 15½×10½×1-inch. They are available in aluminum and steel. Jelly-roll pans are not a good choice for baking individual cookies because the sides interfere with air circulation during baking, resulting in uneven browning.

Loaf pans are designed for baking yeast-bread loaves, quick-bread loaves, pound cakes and fruit cakes. A standard loaf pan measures 9×5×3 inches with slightly flared sides. Smaller loaf pans measuring 8½×4½×2½ inches and miniature pans measuring 5×3×2 inches are also available. Loaf pans come in a variety of materials including aluminum, steel and glass. Pans with dark exteriors are best

for yeast bread. Those with shiny exteriors are best for quick breads and pound cakes.

Muffin pans are rectangular baking pans with 6 or 12 cup-shaped cavities. A standard muffin cup measures 2½ inches in diameter and is 1½ inches deep. Also available are giant muffin pans with cups measuring 3¼ inches in diameter and 2 inches deep and mini pans with cups measuring 1½ to 2 inches in diameter and ¾ inch deep. Muffin pans are made of aluminum, steel or cast iron.

A **pie pan or plate** is exclusively designed for baking a pie. Pie plate generally refers to a glass or ceramic utensil; pie pan refers to a metal utensil. Both are round, about 1½ inches deep and have sloping sides. They range in diameter from 8 to 12 inches. Nine inches is the most popular size. Deep-dish pie pans are 2 inches deep. Glass or dark metal pie pans produce a crisp, golden brown crust. Shiny aluminum pans produce a paler crust.

A **springform pan** is a two-piece round baking pan with an expandable side (secured by a clamp or spring) and a removable bottom. When the clamp is opened, the rim expands and the bottom of the pan can be removed. This makes it easy to remove cheesecakes, cakes and tortes from the pan. The diameter ranges from 6 to 12 inches with 9- and 10-inch pans being the most common.

A **tube pan** is a round baking pan with a hollow tube in the center, which conducts heat to the center of the cake to promote even baking. The tube also supports delicate batters as they rise in the oven. Most tube pans have high, slightly flared sides. Some, such as the angel food cake pan, have a removable bottom. They are generally 8 to 10 inches in diameter and 3½ to 4 inches high with a 12-cup capacity.

Cooling Racks

A cooling rack is a raised wire rack used to cool baked goods. It is raised to allow air circulation around the baked goods or baking pan, which speeds cooling and prevents steam accumulation that results in soggy treats. Choose stable racks that are at least ½ inch high for good circulation,

with the metal wires close together so very small or delicate cookies don't fall between them. Another option is a wire mesh rack (with small square grids) that provides more support and eliminates the problem of cookies slipping between the wires. Cooling racks come in various sizes and are available with a nonstick coating.

Electric Mixers

An electric mixer is not essential, but if you bake often, it does make the process quicker and easier. Stand mixers are considerably more expensive, with a solid base, a heavy-duty motor and several adjustable speeds. They can handle larger quantities of dough and mixtures that are more dense. Hand-held mixers have two removable beaters attached to plastic or metal housing that holds the mixer's motor. They can do most of the operations of stand mixers and offer the convenience of portability, but they sometimes have difficulty with heavy doughs. (They also leave you with only one free hand.)

Food Processors

A food processor can be used for mixing doughs and batters, but it is not always the best tool for this job. Its ability to produce good dough will depend on the age and capacity of the machine, the size of the motor and the sharpness of the blade; you should consult the manufacturer's directions for making dough in the food processor. It does chop, slice, shred and purée very well, however, and in a fraction of the time it takes to do them by hand.

Bread Machines

Bread machines have revolutionized the world of bread baking. It no longer requires a lot of time and effort to make delicious homemade bread—it's now as easy as pressing a button. All bread machines are slightly different, so be sure to read the

manufacturer's instructions. You should know the size of your bread machine before making a loaf of bread. If you are unsure, check the manual or determine the size by measuring how much water the bread pan can hold: a 1½-pound machine can hold about 12 cups of water, and a 2-pound bread machine can hold 13 to 15 cups of water. You can always make a loaf of bread that is smaller than the bread machine's capacity, but you can never make a loaf that is larger than the bread machine's capacity. Once

you know the size of your bread machine, you also need to know what size loaf the recipe makes. If it is not stated in the recipe, use this general rule: a 1½-pound loaf calls for about 3 cups of flour while a 2-pound loaf calls for about 4 cups of

flour. When simply making dough, any size bread machine can be used.

techniques

General Baking Tips

- Adjust the oven racks. Oven racks may need to be set lower for cakes baked in tube pans.

- If two oven racks are used, arrange them so they divide the oven into thirds, then stagger the pans so they are not directly over each other.

- Preheat the oven about 15 minutes before beginning to bake.

- Place the baking pan or sheet on the center rack. If two or more pans are used, allow at least an inch of space between the pans and two inches between the pans and the walls of the oven for proper heat circulation.

- If the heat distribution in your oven is uneven, turn the baking pan or sheet halfway through the baking time.

- Filled pans should be placed in the oven immediately after the batter is mixed. Batter should not sit before baking because chemical leaveners begin working as soon as they are mixed with liquids.

- Avoid opening the oven during the first half of the baking time. The oven temperature must remain constant in order for a cake to rise properly.

- For even baking and browning of cookies, it is best to place only one baking sheet at a time in the center of the oven. However, if you must bake more than one sheet of cookies at a time, rotate them from the top rack to the bottom rack halfway through the baking time.

- Most cookies bake quickly and should be watched carefully to avoid overbaking. Check them at the minimum baking time, then watch carefully to make sure they don't burn. It is generally better to slightly underbake rather than to overbake cookies.

- When reusing the same baking sheets for several batches of cookies, cool the sheets completely before placing more dough on them. Dough will soften and begin to spread on a hot baking sheet.

Temperature

For the best baking results, have all the ingredients you need at room temperature before starting to bake, unless a recipe directs otherwise. This helps create a well-blended, more homogeneous dough.

Butter should be slightly firm—if it is too soft, then the dough will be too soft, and if it is too hard, it will not blend well with the other ingredients. Butter can be softened quickly in the microwave oven if necessary. Place the butter on a microwavable plate and heat it for 15–second intervals at Low (30% power), checking it after each interval. Vegetable shortening and oil can be used immediately if stored at room temperature; they should stand at room temperature for about 15 minutes if they have been stored in the refrigerator.

Remove eggs from the refrigerator about 20 to 30 minutes before baking to allow them to come to room temperature. If you don't have the extra time, you can place the (whole) eggs in a bowl of lukewarm water for several minutes.

Measuring

The first step to successful baking is the careful measuring of ingredients. Unlike regular cooking, baking requires that recipes be followed exactly—a little too much of one ingredient or not enough of another really does make a difference in the final results.

To measure flour, first spoon it into a dry measuring cup until it is mounded over the rim, then level off the top with a straight-edged knife or spatula. Don't shake or tap the measuring cup or press the flour down; this compacts the flour and you may end up with too much, ultimately resulting in dry baked goods. If a recipe calls for "sifted flour," sift the flour before it is measured. If a recipe calls for "flour, sifted," measure the flour first and then sift.

Sugar is measured differently depending on the type of sugar you are using. For granulated sugar, simply dip the measuring cup into the container of sugar, then level off the excess as described above. Brown sugar must be packed down until it is level with the top of the measuring cup for an accurate measurement. To test if you've filled the cup properly, turn it upside down—if the sugar holds its shape, it's been correctly measured. Powdered sugar should be spooned into a measuring cup and leveled off like flour.

To measure liquid ingredients, place a liquid measuring cup on a flat surface and add the liquid until it reaches the correct amount. Make sure you read the measurement line at eye level; reading it from above looks different and will result in an inaccurate measurement.

It is easiest to measure thick, sticky syrups such as corn syrup, maple syrup, molasses and honey in dry measuring cups. Spray the measuring cup with nonstick cooking spray (or lightly grease it with vegetable oil) before measuring so the syrup will slide right out and not stick to the cup.

Stick butter and margarine have measurement markings right on the wrapper. Be sure to look carefully at the markings before cutting the amount you need, because they are not always positioned correctly—sometimes the start of the markings is not aligned with the beginning of the stick. Vegetable shortening should be measured just like brown sugar, packed into a dry measuring cup (to eliminate any air pockets), then leveled off at the top with a straight-edged knife or spatula. Shortening is also sold in packages of 1-cup sticks, with measurement markings on the wrapper similar to butter. Vegetable oil should be measured in liquid measuring cups.

Preparing Pans

Grease baking pans and sheets only if directed to do so in the recipe. It is generally best to use vegetable shortening or nonstick vegetable spray to grease pans because butter and margarine can cause overbrowning at high oven temperatures. When baking pans are greased, the baked goods will have a softer surface. When baking pans are greased and floured, a slight crust will form which helps a tender baked item release from the pan. When baking cookies, avoid overgreasing; this will cause the bottoms to overbrown and the cookies to spread too much. Nonstick cookie sheets should never be greased, even if the recipe calls for greasing, as this can also cause cookies to spread too much.

To **grease** baking pans or sheets, use a paper towel, waxed paper or your fingers to apply a thin, even layer of shortening, or spray lightly with nonstick cooking spray.

To **grease and flour** baking pans or sheets, grease as directed above, then sprinkle flour into the greased pan. Shake or tilt the pan to coat evenly with flour, then tap lightly to remove any excess.

To **line pans** with waxed paper or parchment paper, trace the bottom of the pan onto a piece of waxed or parchment paper and cut it to fit. Grease the pan, but do not flour it. Press the paper onto the bottom of the greased pan. Parchment paper is not recommended for square and rectangular baking pans; however, aluminum foil does an excellent job of keeping pans clean and making bars easy to remove. A quick and easy way to line a baking pan with foil is to invert the pan and shape the foil over the bottom. Lift the shaped foil off and fit it into the upright pan. Make sure there is at least a 2-inch overhang of foil on each side to use as handles for lifting out the bar cookies after baking.

If the recipe calls for a greased baking pan, the foil should be greased (which can be done easily with nonstick cooking spray).

Melting Chocolate

Chocolate is a delicate ingredient, so it is essential to melt it carefully. Bars and chunks of chocolate should always be broken or chopped into small pieces to ensure even melting—this helps retain the flavor and texture of the chocolate. (Small pieces melt quickly and have less chance of burning, while large pieces can melt unevenly, with the surface area overheating before the center melts.) Chop chocolate, a small amount at a time, on a cutting board with a chef's knife. A food processor is not a good tool for chopping chocolate because the heat of the motor can melt the chocolate.

Semisweet and dark chocolate should be stirred frequently during melting, but milk and white chocolate must be stirred almost constantly because the milk solids they contain are very sensitive to heat. The utensils used for melting must be completely dry—any moisture will cause the chocolate to become stiff and grainy (a condition called "seizing"). Never cover chocolate during or after melting; this can result in drops of condensation mixing with the chocolate. If the chocolate does seize, add ½ teaspoon shortening (not butter) for each ounce of chocolate and stir until smooth.

Follow one of these three methods for successful melting.

Double boiler: This is the safest way to melt chocolate. Place the chocolate in the top of a double boiler or in a bowl over hot, not boiling, water; stir gently until the chocolate is smooth. Make sure that the water level in the bottom pot is at least an inch from the bottom of the top pot, and keep the heat low. (Boiling water turns to steam, which will condense and mix with the chocolate, causing it to seize.) When removing the top part of the double boiler, wipe the bottom and

side dry so that no stray drops of water mix with the chocolate when it is transferred to a bowl.

Direct heat: Place the chocolate in a heavy saucepan over very low heat. Stir constantly and remove from the heat as soon as the chocolate is almost melted. Continue stirring until it is completely melted. Use the lowest heat possible and watch the chocolate carefully—it scorches very easily with this method, and once scorched it cannot be used.

Microwave oven: Place 4 to 6 unwrapped 1-ounce squares or 1 cup of chips in a small microwavable bowl. Microwave at Medium (50% power) 2 to 3 minutes, stirring after the first minute and then at 30-second intervals until the chocolate is smooth. (It is important to stir microwaved chocolate between heating intervals because it retains its original shape even when melted, and it can fool you into thinking it is not melting.) To prevent overheating, remove the chocolate from the microwave when it is almost melted, then stir and let any small undissolved lumps finish melting at room temperature.

Chocolate can also be microwaved at High 1 to 1½ minutes, stirring at 30-second intervals until smooth. However, when melting white or milk chocolate, it is safer to use Medium, as these chocolates are more heat-sensitive and can burn very quickly. No matter which level of heat you choose, you should check the chocolate frequently—melting times will vary depending on the wattage of your microwave and the amount of chocolate you are melting.

Testing for Doneness

Oven temperatures can vary significantly depending on the oven model and manufacturer, so watch your baked goods carefully and check for doneness using the test given in the recipe. Begin testing baked goods for doneness 3 to 5 minutes before the end of the specified baking time.

Yeast Breads: the loaf sounds hollow when tapped with your fingers or a wooden spoon

Cakes: a cake tester or toothpick inserted into the center comes out clean and dry; the top springs back when lightly touched

Cheesecakes: a 1-inch area in the center of the cheesecake should jiggle slightly when shaken gently

Fudgelike Bar Cookies: the surface appears dull and a slight imprint remains after touching surface with fingertip

Cakelike Bar Cookies: a toothpick inserted into the center comes out clean and dry

Cookies: the edges are firm and the bottoms are lightly browned

Cooling

- Immediately remove yeast bread from the baking pan or sheet and place it on a wire rack to cool completely. Allowing the bread to cool in the pan will result in a soggy bottom.

- Crisps, cobblers, pies, tarts, bar cookies and brownies can be cooled completely in the baking pan on a wire rack.

- Cool cupcakes, muffins and quick breads in the pan for about 10 to 15 minutes. Then remove them from the pan and let them cool completely on a wire rack.

- Most cakes can be removed from the pan after 10 to 15 minutes of cooling on a wire rack. Two important exceptions are angel food cakes and flourless cakes. Because they have a more delicate structure, they are cooled completely in the pan.

- Angel food cakes and some chiffon cakes are cooled in the pan upside down. An angel food cake pan has three metal feet on which the inverted pan stands for cooling. If you use a tube pan instead, invert the pan on a heatproof funnel or narrow-necked bottle.

- If a cake has cooled too long and will not come out of the pan easily, warm it in a 350°F oven for about 5 minutes. Then, carefully remove it from the pan and let it cool completely on a wire rack.

- Many cookies should be removed from the baking sheets immediately after baking and placed in a single layer on wire racks to cool.

- Fragile cookies may need to cool slightly (1 to 2 minutes) on the baking sheet before being removed to wire racks to cool completely. Follow the instructions given in the recipe.

Storing

- Once yeast bread has cooled completely, wrap it in plastic wrap or place it in an airtight plastic food storage bag. Store the bread at room temperature; placing it in the refrigerator actually causes it to become stale faster. Breads containing milk and fat will last longer than those containing water and no fat.

- Store quick breads in plastic food storage bags or wrapped in plastic at room temperature for up to three days.

- Store one-layer cakes in their baking pans, tightly covered. Store two- or three-layer cakes in a cake-saver or under a large inverted bowl. If the cake has a fluffy or cooked frosting, insert a teaspoon handle under the edge of the cover to prevent an airtight seal and moisture buildup. Cakes with whipped cream frostings or cream fillings should be stored in the refrigerator.

- Meringue-topped pies are best when served the day they are made; refrigerate any leftovers. Refrigerate custard or cream pies immediately after cooling. Fruit pies can be covered and stored at room temperature overnight; refrigerate them for longer storage.

- Store soft and crisp cookies separately at room temperature to prevent changes in texture and flavor. Keep soft cookies in airtight containers. If they begin to dry out, add a piece of apple or bread to the container to help them retain moisture. Store crisp cookies in containers with loose-fitting lids to prevent moisture build-up. If they become soggy, heat undecorated cookies in a 300°F oven for 3 to 5 minutes to restore crispness. Store cookies with sticky glazes, fragile decorations and icings in single layers between sheets of waxed paper.

- Bar cookies and brownies can be stored in their own baking pan, covered with aluminum foil or plastic wrap when cool.

Freezing

- To freeze yeast bread, place the completely cool loaf in the freezer on a flat surface for two hours or until it is solidly frozen. Wrap the frozen loaf in plastic wrap and then in heavy-duty aluminum foil. Label it with the date and the type of bread and return it to the freezer. Bread can be frozen for up to 6 months. Thaw frozen bread in its wrapping at room temperature for 2 to 3 hours. Freshen the loaf by heating it in a preheated 300°F oven for 20 minutes.

- Freeze quick breads sealed in plastic food storage bags or tightly wrapped in heavy-duty foil for up to 3 months. Reheat frozen breads wrapped in foil in a preheated 300°F oven for 15 to 18 minutes.

- Unfrosted cakes can be frozen for up to 4 months if wrapped tightly in plastic wrap. Frosted cakes should be frozen unwrapped until the frosting hardens, then wrapped and sealed. They can be frozen for up to 2 months. Thaw unfrosted cakes, wrapped, at room temperature. For frosted cakes, remove the wrapping and thaw at room temperature or in the refrigerator. Cakes with fruit or custard fillings do not freeze well because they become soggy when thawed.

- To freeze unbaked pies, do not cut steam vents in the top crust. Cover the top with an inverted paper plate for extra protection and package in freezer bags or freezer wrap. To bake, do not thaw. Cut slits in the top crust and allow an additional 15 to 20 minutes of baking time. Baked pies can also be cooled and frozen. To serve, let the pie thaw at room temperature for 2 hours, then heat until warm. Pies with cream or custard fillings and meringue toppings are not recommended for freezing.

- As a rule, crisp cookies freeze better than soft, moist cookies. Rich, buttery bar cookies and brownies are an exception to this rule since they freeze extremely well. Freeze baked cookies in airtight containers or freezer bags for up to 6 months. Thaw cookies unwrapped at room temperature. Meringue-based cookies do not freeze well, and chocolate-dipped cookies will discolor if frozen.

Decorating & Garnishing

Sometimes all it takes is that one special finishing touch to make a dessert go from drab to dazzling. Here are some great ideas for dressing up your baked goods.

Cherry Flower: Cut a maraschino or candied cherry into six wedges, being careful to leave the bottom ⅓ of the cherry uncut. Gently pull out the wedges to make flower petals. Place a tiny piece of candied fruit in the center.

Chocolate Curls: Melt 7 (1-ounce) squares of chocolate; let cool slightly. Pour the melted chocolate onto a cold baking sheet and spread it out, about ¼ inch thick, into a 6×4-inch rectangle. Let the chocolate stand in a cool, dry place until set. (Do not refrigerate.) When the chocolate is just set, use a small metal pancake turner to form the curls. Hold the pancake turner at a 45° angle and scrape the chocolate into a curl. Use a toothpick or wooden skewer to transfer the curl to waxed paper. Store in a cool, dry place until ready to use.

Chocolate-Dipped Garnishes: Dip cookies, nuts or fruit halfway into melted chocolate, then place them on waxed paper until the chocolate is set.

Chocolate Drizzle or Chocolate Shapes: For chocolate drizzle, place melted chocolate in a plastic food storage bag. Snip off a tiny piece of one corner; drizzle over the treat. For chocolate shapes, place a sheet of waxed paper onto an inverted baking sheet. Place melted chocolate in a plastic food storage bag and snip off a tiny piece of one corner. While gently squeezing the bag, guide the opening just above the waxed paper to pipe the chocolate in a steady flow, making the desired shapes. Stop squeezing and then lift the bag at the end of each shape. Let stand in a cool, dry place until the chocolate is set. (Do not refrigerate.) When set, carefully peel the shapes off the waxed paper. Store in a cool, dry place until ready to use.

Chocolate Shavings or Grated Chocolate: Create chocolate shavings by dragging a vegetable peeler across a square of chocolate in short quick strokes. For grated chocolate, working over waxed paper, rub chocolate across the rough surface of a grater, letting the pieces fall onto the waxed paper. The large or small holes of the grater can be used, depending on the size of the chocolate pieces you want.

Citrus Knots: Using a vegetable peeler, remove strips of peel from a lemon, lime or orange. Place the strips on a cutting board. If necessary, scrape the cut sides of the peel with a paring knife to remove any white pith. Cut the strips into 3½×⅛-inch pieces. Tie each piece into a knot.

Citrus Twist: Diagonally cut a lemon, lime or orange into thin slices. Cut a slit through each slice just to the center. Holding each slice with both hands, twist the ends in opposite directions. Place the slices on a plate or the desired food to secure them.

Powdered Sugar or Cocoa Powder: Place the powdered sugar or cocoa powder in a small strainer and gently shake the strainer over the dessert. For fancier designs on cakes, brownies or bar cookies, place a stencil, doily or strips of paper over the top of the dessert before dusting it with sugar or cocoa. Carefully lift off the stencil, doily or paper strips, holding firmly by the edges and pulling straight up.

Powdered Sugar Glazes: Combine 1 cup of sifted powdered sugar and 5 teaspoons of milk in a small bowl. Add ½ teaspoon of vanilla extract or another flavoring, if desired. Stir until smooth. If the glaze is too thin, add additional powdered sugar; if it is too thick, add additional milk, ½ teaspoon at a time. Use the glaze white or tint it with food coloring to fit any occasion.

Strawberry Fan: Place a strawberry on a cutting board with the pointed end facing you. Make four or five lengthwise cuts from just below the stem end of the strawberry to the pointed end. Fan the slices apart slightly, being careful to keep all of the slices attached to the cap.

Sugars, Sprinkles or Candies: Sprinkle cookies with coarse sugar, colored sugars or sprinkles before baking. Or, after baking, cakes and cookies can be frosted and then topped with colored sugar, sprinkles or candies. To decorate a cake, coat the side with sprinkles while the frosting is still soft.

Toasted Coconut or Nuts: Spread coconut or nuts in a thin layer on an ungreased cookie sheet. Bake in a preheated 325°F oven 7 to 10 minutes or until golden, stirring occasionally to promote even browning and prevent burning. Allow coconut and nuts to cool before using. Toasted nuts will darken and become crisper as they cool. To decorate a cake, sprinkle the side with toasted coconut or nuts while the frosting is still soft.

Tinted Coconut: Dilute a few drops of liquid food coloring with ½ teaspoon milk or water in a small bowl. Add 1 to 1⅓ cups flaked coconut and toss with a fork until the coconut is evenly tinted. To decorate a cake, sprinkle the sides with tinted coconut while the frosting is still soft.

fantastic yeast breads

German Rye Beer Bread

1½-Pound Loaf
  1¼ cups light beer, at room temperature
    2 tablespoons light molasses
    1 tablespoon butter
  1½ teaspoons salt
    2 teaspoons caraway seeds
  2½ cups bread flour
    ½ cup rye flour
  1½ teaspoons quick-rise active dry yeast

2-Pound Loaf
  1½ cups light beer, at room temperature
    3 tablespoons light molasses
  1½ tablespoons butter
    2 teaspoons salt
    1 tablespoon caraway seeds
  3¼ cups bread flour
    ¾ cup rye flour
    2 teaspoons quick-rise active dry yeast

Bread Machine Directions

1. Measuring carefully, place all ingredients in bread machine pan in order specified by owner's manual.

2. Program basic cycle and desired crust setting; press start. Remove baked bread from pan; cool on wire rack. *Makes 12 or 16 servings (1 loaf)*

German Rye Beer Bread

Orange Poppy Seed Sweet Rolls

Dough
> 5 tablespoons butter, softened, divided
> ¾ cup orange juice, at room temperature
> 1 egg
> 1 teaspoon salt
> 3 cups bread flour
> ¼ cup granulated sugar
> 1 tablespoon poppy seeds
> 2 teaspoons active dry yeast

Icing
> 1 cup powdered sugar
> 4 teaspoons pulp-free orange juice
> ¾ to 1 teaspoon grated orange peel

Bread Machine Directions

1. Reserve 1 tablespoon butter; cut remaining butter into small pieces. Measuring carefully, place all dough ingredients except reserved butter in bread machine pan in order specified by owner's manual. Program dough cycle setting; press start. (Do not use delay cycle.) Lightly grease 13×9-inch baking pan; set aside.

2. When cycle is complete, remove dough to lightly floured surface. If necessary, knead in additional bread flour to make dough easy to handle. Divide dough into 12 equal pieces. Shape each piece into 10-inch rope; coil each rope and tuck end under coil. Place in prepared pan. Melt reserved 1 tablespoon butter; brush over rolls. Cover with clean towel; let rise in warm, draft-free place 1 to 1½ hours or until doubled in size.

3. Preheat oven to 350°F. Bake rolls 20 minutes or until golden brown. Cool on wire rack.

4. Combine powdered sugar, orange juice and peel in medium bowl until smooth; spread over rolls. *Makes 12 large rolls*

Note: To warm orange juice, place in 2-cup microwavable glass measure and heat at HIGH 10 to 15 seconds or until of desired temperature.

Orange Poppy Seed Sweet Rolls

Triple Chocolate Sticky Buns

Dough
- ¼ cup water
- ½ cup sour cream
- 1 egg
- 3 tablespoons butter, softened
- 1 teaspoon salt
- 2¾ cups bread flour
- ⅓ cup unsweetened cocoa powder
- ¼ cup granulated sugar
- 2 teaspoons active dry yeast

Topping
- ⅓ cup packed light brown sugar
- ¼ cup (½ stick) butter
- 2 tablespoons light corn syrup
- 1 tablespoon unsweetened cocoa powder

Filling
- ⅓ cup packed light brown sugar
- 3 tablespoons butter, softened
- ½ teaspoon ground cinnamon
- ½ cup *each* chocolate chips and coarsely chopped toasted walnuts

Bread Machine Directions

1. Measuring carefully, place all dough ingredients in bread machine pan in order specified by owner's manual. Program dough cycle; press start. (Do not use delay cycle.) Lightly grease 9-inch round cake pan; set aside.

2. Mix topping ingredients in saucepan. Cook and stir over medium heat until sugar is dissolved and mixture bubbles; pour in pan. For filling, mix sugar, butter and cinnamon.

3. When cycle is complete, punch down dough; place on lightly floured surface. If necessary, knead in additional bread flour to make dough easy to handle. Shape into 12×8-inch rectangle. Spread with filling; sprinkle with chips and walnuts. Starting at long side, roll up tightly, jelly-roll fashion; pinch seam to seal. Cut crosswise into 12 slices; arrange over topping in pan. Cover with greased waxed paper. Let rise in warm, draft-free place 45 to 60 minutes or until doubled in size.

4. Place piece of foil on oven rack to catch drippings. Preheat oven to 375°F. Bake about 25 minutes or until buns in center are firm to the touch. *Do not overbake.* Immediately invert onto serving plate.

Makes 12 rolls

Triple Chocolate Sticky Bun

Black Pepper-Onion Bread

1-Pound Loaf
- ⅔ **cup water**
- 1 **tablespoon butter or margarine**
- ¾ **teaspoon salt**
- 2 **cups bread flour**
- 2 **tablespoons nonfat dry milk powder**
- 2 **teaspoons sugar**
- 1 **teaspoon SPICE ISLANDS® Minced Onions**
- ½ **teaspoon SPICE ISLANDS® Medium Grind Java Black Pepper***
- ⅛ **teaspoon SPICE ISLANDS® Garlic Powder**
- 1½ **teaspoons FLEISCHMANN'S® Bread Machine Yeast**

1½-Pound Loaf
- 1 **cup water**
- 1 **tablespoon butter or margarine**
- 1 **teaspoon salt**
- 3 **cups bread flour**
- 3 **tablespoons nonfat dry milk powder**
- 1 **tablespoon sugar**
- 1½ **teaspoons SPICE ISLANDS® Minced Onions**
- ¾ **teaspoon SPICE ISLANDS® Medium Grind Java Black Pepper***
- ¼ **teaspoon SPICE ISLANDS® Garlic Powder**
- 2 **teaspoons FLEISCHMANN'S® Bread Machine Yeast**

If using a finer grind of pepper, reduce the amount to ¼ teaspoon for either loaf size.

Bread Machine Directions

Use the 1-pound recipe if your machine pan holds 10 cups or less of water.
Add ingredients to bread machine pan in the order suggested by manufacturer.
Recommended cycle: Basic/white bread cycle; medium/normal crust color setting.
Timed-bake feature can be used.   *Makes 1 loaf (8 or 12 slices)*

Black Pepper-Onion Bread

Cinnamon-Nut Bubble Ring

Dough
>   ¾ cup apple juice, at room temperature
>   1 egg
>   2 tablespoons butter, softened
>   1 teaspoon salt
>   3 cups bread flour
>   ½ cup finely chopped walnuts
>   ¼ cup granulated sugar
>   2 tablespoons nonfat dry milk powder
>   ¼ teaspoon ground cinnamon
>   2 teaspoons active dry yeast

Cinnamon Coating
>   ½ cup granulated sugar
>   4 teaspoons ground cinnamon
>   3 tablespoons butter, melted

Apple Glaze
>   1 cup powdered sugar
>   4 to 5 teaspoons apple juice

Bread Machine Directions

1. Measuring carefully, place all dough ingredients in bread machine pan in order specified by owner's manual. Program dough cycle setting; press start. (Do not use delay cycle.) Lightly grease 10-inch tube pan; set aside.

2. When cycle is complete, remove dough to lightly floured surface. If necessary, knead in additional bread flour to make dough easy to handle. For cinnamon coating, combine granulated sugar and cinnamon in shallow bowl. Shape dough into 2-inch balls. Roll in melted butter; coat evenly with cinnamon-sugar mixture. Place in prepared pan. Cover with clean towel; let rise in warm, draft-free place 1 to 1½ hours or until doubled in size.

3. Preheat oven to 350°F. Bake bread 30 minutes or until golden brown. Let cool in pan on wire rack 10 minutes; carefully remove from pan. Cool completely.

4. For apple glaze, combine powdered sugar and apple juice in medium bowl until smooth; drizzle over bubble ring. *Makes 12 servings*

Note: To warm apple juice, place in 2-cup microwavable glass measure and heat at HIGH 10 to 15 seconds or until of desired temperature.

Cinnamon-Nut Bubble Ring

Pumpernickel Raisin Bread

        **3 tablespoons plus 1 teaspoon GRANDMA'S® Gold Molasses,
            divided**
        2 packages (¼ ounce each) active dry yeast
    1¼ cups warm water (105° to 115°F), divided
        2 cups all-purpose flour
        1 cup rye flour
        2 tablespoons unsweetened cocoa powder
        2 teaspoons salt
        2 teaspoons caraway seeds
    1½ cups golden raisins

Glaze
        1 tablespoon GRANDMA'S® Gold Molasses
        1 tablespoon water
        2 tablespoons caraway seeds

1. Dissolve 1 teaspoon Grandma's® Gold Molasses and yeast in ¼ cup warm water in small bowl. Let stand until foamy, about 5 minutes.

2. Combine flours, cocoa, salt and 2 teaspoons caraway seeds in 12-cup food processor fitted with dough or steel blade. Add yeast mixture; mix well. Mix remaining 1 cup warm water and 3 tablespoons Grandma's® Gold Molasses in medium bowl.

3. With machine running, pour molasses mixture slowly through feed tube. When dough forms a ball, process 1 minute. If dough sticks to side of bowl, add additional all-purpose flour, 2 tablespoons at a time. If dough is too dry and does not stick together, add water, 1 tablespoon at a time.

4. Place dough in large greased bowl and turn to coat. Bring large shallow pot of water to a simmer. Remove from heat; place wire rack in pot. Place bowl with dough on rack; cover with towel. Let rise 1 to 1¼ hours or until doubled in bulk.

5. Punch dough down; flatten to ¼-inch thickness. Sprinkle with raisins; roll up dough and knead several times. Shape into 8-inch round; place on greased baking sheet. Place on rack over hot water as directed above; cover with towel. Let rise 1 to 1¼ hours or until doubled in bulk.

6. For glaze, combine 1 tablespoon Grandma's® Gold Molasses and 1 tablespoon water. Brush over loaf; sprinkle with 2 tablespoons caraway seeds.

7. Bake in 350°F oven 25 to 30 minutes until bread sounds hollow when tapped. Cool on rack 30 minutes.   *Makes 1 large loaf*

Sourdough Herb Bread

Sourdough Starter
  ½ **cup warm water (105° to 115°F)**
  1 **teaspoon active dry yeast**
  1 **teaspoon sugar**
  ½ **cup bread flour**

Dough
  ¾ **cup water**
    Sourdough Starter
  1 **tablespoon vegetable oil**
 1¼ **teaspoons salt**
  3 **cups bread flour**
  2 **teaspoons sugar**
  2 **teaspoons dried basil leaves**
  1 **teaspoon dried oregano leaves**
  ½ **teaspoon dried thyme leaves**
  ¼ **to** ½ **teaspoon dried rosemary**
  1 **teaspoon active dry yeast**

Bread Machine Directions

1. For sourdough starter, combine water, yeast and sugar in small bowl, stirring until yeast is dissolved. Let stand 10 minutes. Stir in bread flour until smooth. Let mixture stand, uncovered, at room temperature 12 to 24 hours.

2. For dough, measuring carefully, place all ingredients in bread machine pan in order specified by owner's manual.

3. Program basic cycle and desired crust setting; press start. Immediately remove baked bread from pan; cool on wire rack.   *Makes 1 (1½-pound) loaf*

Focaccia

1 cup water
1 tablespoon olive oil, plus additional for brushing
1 teaspoon salt
1 tablespoon sugar
3 cups bread flour
2¼ teaspoons (1 packet) RED STAR® Active Dry Yeast or QUICK•RISE™ Yeast or Bread Machine Yeast
    Suggested toppings: sun-dried tomatoes, roasted bell pepper slices, sautéed onion rings, fresh and dried herbs in any combination, grated hard cheese

Bread Machine Method

Place room temperature ingredients, except toppings, in pan in order listed. Select dough cycle. Check dough consistency after 5 minutes of kneading, making adjustments if necessary.

Hand-Held Mixer Method

Combine yeast, 1 cup flour, sugar and salt. Combine water and 1 tablespoon oil; heat mixture to 120° to 130°F. Combine dry and liquid mixtures in mixing bowl on low speed. Beat 2 to 3 minutes on medium speed. By hand, stir in enough remaining flour to make a firm dough. Knead on floured surface 5 to 7 minutes or until smooth and elastic. Add additional flour, if necessary.

Stand Mixer Method

Combine yeast, 1 cup flour, sugar and salt. Combine water and 1 tablespoon oil; heat mixture to 120° to 130°F. Combine dry and liquid mixtures in mixing bowl with paddle or beaters for 4 minutes on medium speed. Gradually add remaining flour and knead with dough hook 5 to 7 minutes or until smooth and elastic. Add additional flour, if necessary.

Food Processor Method

In 2-cup measure, heat ¼ cup water to 110° to 115°F; keep remaining ¾ cup water cold. Add yeast; set aside. Insert dough blade in work bowl; add bread flour, sugar and salt. Pulse to combine. Add cold water and olive oil to yeast mixture; stir to combine. With machine running, add liquid mixture through feed tube in a steady stream only as fast as flour will absorb it. Open lid to check dough consistency. If dough is stiff and somewhat dry, add 1 teaspoon water; if soft and sticky, add

continued on page 58

Focaccia

Focaccia, continued

1 tablespoon flour. Close lid and process for 10 seconds. Check dough consistency again, making additional adjustments if necessary.

Rising, Shaping, and Baking

Place dough in lightly oiled bowl and turn to grease top. Cover; let rise until dough tests ripe.* Turn dough onto lightly floured surface; punch down to remove air bubbles. On lightly floured surface, shape dough into a ball. Place on greased baking sheet. Flatten to 14-inch circle. With knife, cut circle in dough about 1 inch from edge, cutting almost through to baking sheet. Pierce center with fork. Cover; let rise about 15 minutes. Brush with oil and sprinkle with desired toppings. Bake in preheated 375°F oven 25 to 30 minutes or until golden brown. Remove from baking sheet to cool. Serve warm or at room temperature.   *Makes 1 (14-inch) loaf*

Place two fingers into the dough and then remove them. If the holes remain the dough is ripe and ready to punch down.

Note: When flattening dough into circle, if the dough does not stretch easily, let it rest a couple of minutes and then press it out. Repeat if necessary.

Sugar & Spice Bread

   1 cup water
   ¼ cup (½ stick) butter, softened
   1 teaspoon salt
   3 cups bread flour
   ¼ cup nonfat dry milk powder
   ¼ cup packed light brown sugar
   2 teaspoons ground cinnamon
   ¼ to ½ teaspoon ground nutmeg
   ⅛ to ¼ teaspoon ground cloves
   2 teaspoons active dry yeast

Bread Machine Directions

1. Measuring carefully, place all ingredients in bread machine pan in order specified by owner's manual.

2. Program basic cycle and desired crust setting; press start. Immediately remove baked bread from pan; cool on wire rack.   *Makes 1 (1½-pound) loaf*

Note: The spicy-sweet flavor of this loaf makes it a wonderful breakfast bread. The flavor is especially good when the bread is served toasted.

Sugar & Spice Bread

Pecan Cinnamon Rolls

1 package (¼ ounce) active dry yeast
1 cup warm water (105° to 115°F)
½ cup plus 2 tablespoons honey, divided
⅓ cup nonfat dry milk powder
1 egg, lightly beaten
1½ cups bread flour
1 teaspoon salt
3 tablespoons butter, melted and cooled
1 cup whole-wheat pastry flour
1 to 1½ cups oat flour or barley flour
½ cup chopped pecans
3 tablespoons butter, softened
¼ cup firmly packed light brown sugar
2 teaspoons ground cinnamon

1. Sprinkle yeast over water in large bowl; stir to dissolve. Add 2 tablespoons honey, milk powder and egg; stir. Add bread flour, a little at a time, stirring after each addition. Beat mixture 100 times or until very smooth, using large spoon to stretch mixture up to incorporate air. Let dough rest, covered, 10 to 15 minutes.

2. Fold salt and 3 tablespoons melted butter into dough. (Do not cut or tear dough, as this will lessen elasticity and rising ability.) Sprinkle dough with remaining flours, 1 cup at a time, folding wet mixture from side of bowl over top of flours. Continue folding in flour until dough is thick and heavy and does not stick to side of bowl. Turn dough out onto lightly floured surface. Scrape bowl clean; add scrapings to dough.

3. Knead dough with floured hands until smooth and elastic, 10 to 15 minutes, adding small amounts of flour as needed to prevent sticking. Shape dough into a ball; place in large greased bowl. Turn dough over. Cover with clean, damp towel. Let rise in warm, draft-free place about 1 hour or until doubled in size.

4. Meanwhile, spread remaining ½ cup honey evenly in bottom of 9×9×2-inch baking pan; sprinkle with pecans. Set aside.

5. Turn dough out onto lightly floured surface. Punch down dough. Shape dough into ¼-inch-thick rectangle; spread with 3 tablespoons softened butter. Sprinkle with brown sugar and cinnamon. Roll up into log; cut log into 9 equal pieces. Place rolls in pan. Cover with clean, damp towel; let rise 20 to 30 minutes.

6. Preheat oven to 350°F. Bake about 30 minutes or until golden brown and rolls sound hollow when tapped. Cool slightly; invert onto plate. *Makes 9 rolls*

Pecan Cinnamon Roll

Southwest Sausage Bread

1 package active dry yeast
1 tablespoon sugar
1 cup warm water (105° to 115°F)
1¾ to 2¼ cups all-purpose flour, divided
1½ cups whole wheat flour, divided
1 egg
2 tablespoons vegetable oil
¼ teaspoon salt
1 medium onion, finely chopped
4 ounces dry chorizo or pepperoni sausage, chopped
1 cup (4 ounces) shredded Monterey Jack cheese

1. Sprinkle yeast and sugar over warm water in large bowl; stir until dissolved. Let stand 5 minutes or until bubbly. Add 1 cup all-purpose flour, 1 cup whole wheat flour, egg, oil and salt. Beat until blended. Beat 3 minutes. Stir in remaining whole-wheat flour and enough all-purpose flour, about ¾ cup, to make soft dough.

2. Sprinkle work surface with all-purpose flour. Turn out dough onto floured surface; flatten. Knead 5 to 8 minutes or until smooth and elastic; gradually add remaining ½ cup all-purpose flour to prevent sticking, if necessary. Shape into ball; place in lightly greased bowl. Turn dough over. Cover; let rise in warm, draft-free place 1 hour or until doubled in size.

3. Cook onion and sausage in skillet over medium heat 5 minutes or until onion is tender. Drain on paper towels.

4. Punch down dough. Knead on floured surface 1 minute. Cover; let rest 10 minutes. Spray 9×5-inch loaf pan with nonstick cooking spray. Roll dough into 24×11-inch rectangle. Sprinkle sausage mixture and cheese over dough. Roll up dough jelly-roll style from short end. Pinch seam and ends to seal. Cut dough lengthwise into halves. With cut sides up, twist halves together. Pinch ends to seal. Place in pan, cut sides up. Let rise 1 hour or until doubled in size.

5. Preheat oven to 375°F. Bake 30 minutes or until loaf sounds hollow when tapped. Remove immediately from pan. Cool 30 minutes on wire rack.

Makes 12 servings

Southwest Sausage Bread

Freezer Rolls

1¼ cups warm water (100° to 110°F)
2 envelopes FLEISCHMANN'S® Active Dry Yeast
½ cup sugar
½ cup warm milk (100° to 110°F)
⅓ cup butter or margarine, softened
1½ teaspoons salt
5½ to 6 cups all-purpose flour
2 eggs

Place ½ cup warm water in large warm bowl. Sprinkle yeast over water; stir until dissolved. Add remaining ¾ cup warm water, sugar, milk, butter, salt and 2 cups flour. Beat 2 minutes at medium speed of electric mixer. Add eggs and ½ cup flour. Beat at high speed for 2 minutes. Stir in enough remaining flour to make soft dough. Turn out onto lightly floured surface. Knead until smooth and elastic, about 8 to 10 minutes. Cover with plastic wrap; let rest for 20 minutes.

Punch dough down. Shape into desired shapes for dinner rolls. Place on greased baking sheets. Cover with plastic wrap and foil, sealing well. Freeze up to 1 week.*

Once frozen, rolls may be placed in plastic freezer bags.

Remove rolls from freezer; unwrap and place on greased baking sheets. Cover; let rise in warm, draft-free place until doubled in size, about 1½ hours.

Bake at 350°F for 15 minutes or until done. Remove from baking sheets; cool on wire racks. *Makes about 2 dozen rolls*

*To bake without freezing: After shaping, let rise in warm, draft-free place until doubled in size, about 1 hour. Bake according to above directions.

Shaping the Dough: Crescents: Divide dough in half. Roll each half to 14-inch circle. Cut each into 12 pie-shaped wedges. Roll up tightly from wide end. Curve ends slightly to form crescents; **Knots:** Divide dough into 24 equal pieces; roll each to 9-inch rope. Tie once loosely. **Coils:** Divide dough into 24 equal pieces; roll each to 9-inch rope. Coil each rope and tuck end under coil. **Twists:** Divide dough into 24 equal pieces; roll each into 12-inch rope. Fold each rope in half and twist three to four times. Pinch ends to seal.

Freezer Rolls

Pizza Breadsticks

     1 cup water
     1 tablespoon olive oil
     1 teaspoon salt
     3 cups all-purpose flour
     ½ cup (2 ounces) shredded mozzarella cheese
     ¼ cup shredded Parmesan cheese
     ¼ cup chopped red bell pepper
     1 green onion with top, sliced
     1 clove garlic, minced
     ½ teaspoon dried basil leaves
     ½ teaspoon dried oregano leaves
     ¼ teaspoon red pepper flakes (optional)
  1½ teaspoons active dry yeast

Bread Machine Directions

1. Measuring carefully, place all ingredients in bread machine pan in order specified by owner's manual. Program dough cycle setting; press start. Grease large baking sheets; set aside.

2. When cycle is complete, remove dough to lightly floured surface. If necessary, knead in additional all-purpose flour to make dough easy to handle. Roll dough into 14×8-inch rectangle. Let dough rest 5 minutes. Cut dough crosswise into 28 (8×½-inch) strips. Twist each strip 3 to 4 times; place 2 inches apart on prepared baking sheets, pressing both ends to baking sheet. Cover with clean towels; let rise in warm, draft-free place 30 minutes or until doubled in size.

3. Preheat oven to 425°F. Bake 15 to 20 minutes or until golden brown. Cool on wire racks.   *Makes 28 breadsticks*

tip

Serve these delicious breadsticks with your favorite pasta sauce on the side for dipping.

Pizza Breadsticks

Dinner Rolls

1½ Pounds Dough
- ¾ cup milk
- 1 egg
- ⅓ cup shortening
- 1 teaspoon salt
- 3 cups all-purpose flour
- 3 tablespoons sugar
- 1½ teaspoons active dry yeast

2 Pounds Dough
- 1 cup milk
- 2 eggs
- ½ cup shortening
- 1½ teaspoons salt
- 4 cups all-purpose flour
- ¼ cup sugar
- 2 teaspoons active dry yeast

Bread Machine Directions

1. Measuring carefully, place all ingredients in bread machine pan in order specified by owner's manual. Program dough cycle setting; press start. For 1½ pounds dough, grease 13×9-inch baking pan; set aside. For 2 pounds dough, grease 2 (8-inch) square baking pans; set aside.

2. When cycle is complete, remove dough to lightly floured surface. If necessary, knead in additional flour to make dough easy to handle. For 1½ pounds dough, divide into 18 equal pieces; for 2 pounds dough, divide into 24 equal pieces. Shape each dough piece into smooth ball. Place in prepared pan(s). Cover with clean towel; let rise in warm, draft-free place 45 minutes or until doubled in size.

3. Preheat oven to 375°F. Bake 15 to 20 minutes or until golden brown. Remove from pan(s); cool on wire rack(s). *Makes 18 to 24 rolls*

Golden Cheddar Batter Bread

    1 package active dry yeast
   ¾ cup warm water (110° to 115°F)
    3 cups unsifted all-purpose flour, divided
1½ cups finely chopped Golden Delicious apples
    1 cup shredded Cheddar cheese
    2 eggs, lightly beaten
    2 tablespoons sugar
    2 tablespoons vegetable shortening
    1 teaspoon salt
     Buttery Apple Spread (recipe follows)

1. In large bowl, combine yeast and water, stirring to dissolve yeast. Set aside until mixture begins to foam, about 5 minutes. Add 1½ cups flour, apples, cheese, eggs, sugar, shortening and salt to yeast mixture; beat with electric mixer at medium speed 2 minutes. Stir in remaining flour gradually with spoon. Cover with clean cloth and let rise 50 to 60 minutes or until doubled. Meanwhile, prepare Buttery Apple Spread.

2. Grease 9×5-inch loaf pan. Beat batter by hand 30 seconds. Spread batter evenly in prepared pan. Cover with cloth and let rise 40 minutes or until nearly doubled.

3. Heat oven to 375°F. Bake bread 45 to 55 minutes or until loaf sounds hollow when gently tapped. Remove from pan; cool on wire rack at least 15 minutes. Serve with Buttery Apple Spread. *Makes 1 loaf*

Buttery Apple Spread: Peel, core and slice 1 Golden Delicious apple; place in small saucepan with 1 tablespoon water. Cover tightly and cook over medium heat until apple is very tender. Mash apple with fork; cool completely. In small bowl, beat ½ cup softened butter with electric mixer until light and fluffy. Gradually add mashed apple; beat until well blended. Makes about 1 cup.

*Favorite recipe from **Washington Apple Commission***

Thyme-Cheese Bubble Loaf

1 package active dry yeast
1 teaspoon sugar
1 cup warm water (105° to 115°F)
3 cups all-purpose flour
1 teaspoon salt
2 tablespoons vegetable oil
1 cup (4 ounces) shredded Monterey Jack cheese
4 tablespoons butter, melted
¼ cup chopped fresh parsley
3 teaspoons finely chopped fresh thyme or ¾ teaspoon dried thyme leaves, crushed

1. Sprinkle yeast and sugar over warm water in small bowl; stir until dissolved. Let stand 5 minutes or until bubbly.

2. Combine flour and salt in food processor. With food processor running, add yeast mixture and oil. Process until mixture forms dough that leaves side of bowl. If dough is too dry, add 1 to 2 tablespoons water. If dough is too wet, add 1 to 2 tablespoons additional flour until dough leaves side of bowl. Dough will be sticky.

3. Place dough in large greased bowl. Turn dough over. Cover with towel; let rise in warm, draft-free place about 1 hour or until doubled in size.

4. Punch down dough. Knead cheese into dough on lightly floured surface until evenly distributed. Cover with towel; let rest 10 minutes.

5. Grease 1½-quart casserole dish or 8½×4½-inch loaf pan; set aside. Combine butter, parsley and thyme in small bowl.

6. Roll out dough into 8×6-inch rectangle with lightly floured rolling pin. Cut dough into 48 (1-inch) squares; shape into balls. Dip into parsley mixture. Place in prepared dish.

7. Cover with towel; let rise in warm place about 45 minutes or until doubled in size. Preheat oven to 375°F.

8. Bake 35 to 40 minutes or until top is golden and loaf sounds hollow when tapped. Immediately remove from casserole dish; cool on wire rack 30 minutes. Serve warm. Store leftover bread in refrigerator. *Makes 1 loaf*

Thyme-Cheese Bubble Loaf

Garlic and Herb Parmesan Buns

8 Buns
- 1¼ cups water
- 1 tablespoon sugar
- 1½ teaspoons salt
- 1 teaspoon garlic powder
- 2 teaspoons dried Italian herbs
- ⅓ cup grated Parmesan cheese
- 3 cups bread flour
- 1 tablespoon quick-rise active dry yeast

12 Buns
- 1½ cups water
- 2 tablespoons sugar
- 2 teaspoons salt
- 1½ teaspoons garlic powder
- 1 tablespoon dried Italian herbs
- ½ cup grated Parmesan cheese
- 4 cups bread flour
- 1 tablespoon quick-rise active dry yeast

Topping
- 1 to 2 tablespoons grated Parmesan cheese

Bread Machine Directions

1. Measuring carefully, place all ingredients except topping in bread machine pan in order specified by owner's manual. Program dough cycle setting; press start.

2. Turn out dough onto lightly greased surface. Cut dough into 8 or 12 pieces. Shape into smooth balls. Place on greased baking sheet; flatten slightly. Let rise in warm, draft-free place 45 minutes or until doubled in size.

3. Preheat oven to 400°F. Brush buns with water; sprinkle tops with pinch of cheese. Bake 15 minutes or until lightly browned. Serve warm or transfer to wire racks to cool completely.
Makes 8 or 12 buns

Garlic and Herb Parmesan Buns

Basic White Bread

2 packages active dry yeast
2 tablespoons sugar
2 cups warm water (105°F to 115°F)
6 to 6½ cups all-purpose flour, divided
½ cup nonfat dry milk powder
2 tablespoons shortening
2 teaspoons salt

1. Sprinkle yeast and sugar over warm water in small bowl; stir until dissolved. Let stand 5 minutes or until bubbly.

2. Add 3 cups flour, milk powder, shortening and salt. Beat with electric mixer at low speed until blended. Increase speed to medium; beat 2 minutes. Stir in enough additional flour, about 3 cups, to make soft dough. Turn out onto lightly floured surface. Knead about 10 minutes adding enough of remaining flour to make dough smooth and elastic.

3. Shape dough into ball; place in large greased bowl. Turn dough over. Cover with towel; let rise in warm, draft-free place about 1 hour or until doubled in size.

4. Punch down dough; knead on lightly floured surface 1 minute. Cover with towel; let rest 10 minutes.

5. Grease 2 (8½×4½-inch) loaf pans; set aside. Divide dough in half. Roll out half of dough into 12×8-inch rectangle with lightly floured rolling pin. Starting with 1 short side, roll up dough jelly-roll style. Pinch seam and ends to seal. Place loaf, seam side down, in prepared pan, tucking ends under. Repeat with remaining dough.

6. Cover and let rise in warm place 1 hour or until doubled in size.

7. Preheat oven to 375°F. Bake 30 to 35 minutes or until loaves are golden brown and sound hollow when tapped. Immediately remove from pans; cool completely on wire racks.
Makes 2 loaves

Refrigerator White Bread: Prepare and shape dough as directed in steps 1 through 5. Spray 2 sheets of plastic wrap with nonstick cooking spray. Cover dough with plastic wrap, greased side down. Refrigerate 3 to 24 hours. Dough should rise to top of pans during refrigeration. Remove loaves from refrigerator 20 minutes before baking. Preheat oven to 375°F. Remove plastic wrap. Bake 45 to 50 minutes or until loaves are golden brown and sound hollow when tapped. Immediately remove from pans; cool completely on wire racks.

Basic White Bread

Honey Wheat Brown-and-Serve Rolls

2 packages active dry yeast
1 teaspoon sugar
¾ cup warm water (105°F to 115°F)
2 cups whole wheat flour
2 cups all-purpose flour
¼ cup shortening
¼ cup honey
1 egg
1 teaspoon salt
Additional ¼ to 1 cup all-purpose flour

1. Sprinkle yeast and sugar over warm water in small bowl; stir until dissolved. Let stand 5 minutes or until bubbly. Combine whole wheat flour and 2 cups all-purpose flour in medium bowl. Measure 1½ cups flour mixture into large bowl. Add yeast mixture, shortening, honey, egg and salt. Beat with electric mixer at low speed until smooth. Increase mixer speed to medium; beat 2 minutes. Reduce speed to low; beat in 1 cup flour mixture. Increase mixer speed to medium; beat 2 minutes. Stir in remaining flour mixture and enough additional all-purpose flour, beginning with ¼ cup, to make a soft dough.

2. Turn dough out onto lightly floured surface. Knead 8 to 10 minutes or until smooth and elastic, adding more flour to prevent sticking, if necessary. Shape dough into a ball; place in large greased bowl. Turn dough over. Cover with clean towel. Let rise in warm, draft-free place about 1½ hours or until doubled in size. Punch down dough. Turn dough out onto lightly floured surface. Knead dough briefly; cover and let rest 15 minutes. Meanwhile, grease 24 muffin pan cups.

3. Divide dough into 24 pieces; cut each piece into thirds. Roll each third into a ball. Place 3 balls in each prepared muffin cup. Cover and let rise in warm place about 30 minutes or until doubled in size.

4. Preheat oven to 275°F.* Bake 20 to 25 minutes or until rolls are set but not brown. Immediately remove rolls from muffin cups and cool completely on wire racks. Store in resealable plastic food storage bags in refrigerator or freezer.

5. To bake rolls, thaw if frozen. Preheat oven to 400°F. Grease large jelly-roll pan. Place rolls on prepared pan. Bake 8 to 10 minutes or until golden brown.

Makes 24 rolls

*To bake and serve rolls immediately, preheat oven to 375°F. Bake 15 to 20 minutes or until golden brown. Immediately remove from pan. Serve warm.

Honey Wheat Brown-and-Serve Rolls

incredible coffee cakes

Peanut Butter Coffee Cake

1½ cups packed brown sugar, divided
2½ cups all-purpose flour, divided
¾ cup JIF® Creamy Peanut Butter, divided
2 tablespoons butter or margarine, melted
¼ cup CRISCO® all-vegetable shortening
2 eggs
2 teaspoons baking powder
½ teaspoon salt
½ teaspoon baking soda
1 cup milk

1. Preheat oven to 375°F.

2. Combine ½ cup brown sugar, ½ cup flour, ¼ cup JIF® peanut butter and melted butter until crumbly; set aside.

3. Cream remaining ½ cup JIF® peanut butter and shortening. Slowly beat in remaining 1 cup brown sugar. Add eggs, 1 at a time, beating until fluffy.

4. Combine remaining 2 cups flour, baking powder, salt and baking soda; mix well. Add flour mixture alternately with milk to creamed mixture, beating after each addition.

5. Spread batter in greased 13×9×2-inch baking pan. Top with crumbly mixture. Bake for 30 to 35 minutes or until toothpick inserted into center comes out clean. Cool completely. Garnish as desired. *Makes 16 to 18 servings*

Peanut Butter Coffee Cake

Berry-Cheese Braid

Dough
- 1 cup milk
- 1 egg, lightly beaten
- 3 tablespoons butter, softened
- 1 teaspoon salt
- 3 cups bread flour
- 5 tablespoons sugar
- 1½ teaspoons active dry yeast

Filling
- 1 package (8 ounces) cream cheese, softened
- 1 egg
- ¼ cup sugar
- ½ teaspoon vanilla
- 1 cup *each* fresh raspberries and fresh blueberries

Topping
- 1 tablespoon sugar

Bread Machine Directions

1. Measuring carefully, place all dough ingredients in bread machine pan in order specified by owner's manual. Program dough cycle setting; press start. (Do not use delay cycle.) Lightly grease 2 baking sheets; set aside.

2. For filling, beat cream cheese, egg, sugar and vanilla in large bowl until blended.

3. When cycle is complete, remove dough to lightly floured surface. If necessary, knead in additional bread flour to make dough easy to handle. Divide dough in half. Roll each half into 12×9-inch* rectangle; place rectangles on prepared baking sheets.

4. Spread filling lengthwise down center third of each dough rectangle, leaving 1-inch border at short ends. Sprinkle evenly with raspberries and blueberries. Fold 1-inch dough borders in toward centers. Make 5 cuts on each long side of dough rectangles, just up to filling, to form 6 strips on each side. Gently fold strips in toward centers, alternating left and right, and allowing some filling to show through. Sprinkle braids with 1 tablespoon sugar. Cover with clean towels; let rise in warm, draft-free place 45 minutes or until doubled in size.

5. Preheat oven to 325°F. Bake braids 25 to 30 minutes or until golden brown. Remove from baking sheets; cool on wire racks.   *Makes 2 braids or 24 servings*

For a slightly flatter appearance, roll dough into 14×9-inch rectangle.

Berry-Cheese Braid

Chocolate Chip Coffeecake

3 cups all-purpose flour, divided
⅓ cup sugar
2 envelopes FLEISCHMANN'S® RapidRise™ Yeast
1 teaspoon salt
½ cup milk
½ cup water
½ cup butter or margarine
2 eggs
¾ cup semi-sweet chocolate morsels
Chocolate Nut Topping (recipe follows)

In large bowl, combine 1 cup flour, sugar, undissolved yeast and salt. Heat milk, water and butter until very warm (120° to 130°F). Gradually add to dry ingredients. Beat 2 minutes at medium speed of electric mixer, scraping bowl occasionally. Add eggs and 1 cup flour; beat 2 minutes at high speed, scraping bowl occasionally. Stir in chocolate morsels and remaining flour to make a soft batter. Turn into greased 13×9×2-inch baking pan. Cover; let rise in warm, draft-free place until doubled in size, about 1 hour.

Bake at 400°F for 15 minutes; remove from oven and sprinkle with Chocolate Nut Topping. Return to oven and bake additional 10 minutes or until done. Cool in pan for 10 minutes. Remove from pan; cool on wire rack. *Makes 1 cake*

Chocolate Nut Topping: In medium bowl, cut ½ cup butter into ⅔ cup all-purpose flour until crumbly. Stir in ⅔ cup sugar, 2 teaspoons ground cinnamon, 1 cup semi-sweet chocolate morsels and 1 cup chopped pecans.

tip

One package of active dry yeast contains thousands of microscopic living plants that are activated by warm liquid and fed by sugar and starch. Yeast releases carbon dioxide gas bubbles that cause doughs and batters to rise. Store packages of active dry yeast in a cool, dry place.

Chocolate Chip Coffeecake

Cranberry-Pecan Wreath

½ cup milk
1 egg
¼ cup butter or margarine, cut up
½ teaspoon salt
2½ cups bread flour
¼ cup sugar
2 teaspoons FLEISCHMANN'S® Bread Machine Yeast
Cranberry-Pecan Filling (recipe follows)
Orange Glaze (recipe follows)

Bread Machine Directions

Add all ingredients except filling and glaze to bread machine pan in the order suggested by manufacturer. Select dough/manual cycle. When cycle is complete, remove dough to floured surface. If necessary, knead in enough flour to make dough easy to handle. Roll dough to 26×6-inch rectangle; spread Cranberry-Pecan Filling over dough to within ½ inch of edges. Beginning at long end, roll up tightly as for jelly roll. Pinch seam to seal. Form into ring; join ends, pinching to seal. Transfer to greased large baking sheet. Cover and let rise in warm, draft-free place until doubled in size, about 45 to 60 minutes.

Bake at 350°F for 30 to 35 minutes or until done. Remove from pan; cool on wire rack. Drizzle with Orange Glaze; decorate with additional cranberries, orange slices and pecan halves, if desired. *Makes 1 (8-inch) coffeecake*

Cranberry-Pecan Filling: In medium saucepan, combine 1 cup finely chopped fresh or frozen cranberries, ⅔ cup firmly packed brown sugar and ¼ cup butter or margarine. Bring to a boil over medium-high heat. Reduce heat and simmer 4 to 6 minutes or until very thick, stirring frequently. Remove mixture from heat; stir in ½ cup toasted chopped pecans.

Orange Glaze: In small bowl, cream 1½ tablespoons butter or margarine with 1 cup sifted powdered sugar. Add 1 to 2 tablespoons milk and 1½ teaspoons freshly grated orange peel. Stir until smooth.

Cranberry-Pecan Wreath

Sour Cream Coffee Cake

Cranberry Sauce (recipe follows)
Streusel Topping (recipe follows)
¾ **cup sugar**
6 **tablespoons butter**
2 **eggs**
1 **cup sour cream**
1 **tablespoon grated lemon peel**
1½ **teaspoons vanilla**
1½ **cups all-purpose flour**
1½ **teaspoons ground cardamom**
1 **teaspoon** *each* **baking powder and baking soda**
⅛ **teaspoon salt**

1. Prepare Cranberry Sauce; set aside. Prepare Streusel Topping; set aside. Grease and flour 8-inch springform pan. Preheat oven to 350°F.

2. Beat sugar and butter in large bowl until light and fluffy. Beat in eggs, 1 at a time, until well blended. Beat in sour cream, lemon peel and vanilla. Add flour, cardamom, baking powder, baking soda and salt; beat just until blended.

3. Spoon half of batter into prepared pan. Sprinkle half of streusel over batter. Repeat layers ending with streusel. Bake 50 to 60 minutes or until toothpick inserted in center comes out clean. Cool in pan on wire rack 15 minutes.

4. Run knife around edge of pan to loosen cake. Remove side of pan. Cool until cake is just warm. Transfer cake to serving plate. Serve with Cranberry Sauce.

Makes 10 servings

Cranberry Sauce: Combine 2 cups fresh cranberries, 1 cup orange juice and ¾ cup sugar in saucepan. Bring to a boil over high heat, stirring frequently; reduce heat to medium-low. Cover; simmer 10 minutes or until cranberries are tender and pop. Remove saucepan from heat. Reserve ½ of cranberries in small bowl. Mash remaining cranberries in saucepan. Blend 2 teaspoons cornstarch and 2 teaspoons water until smooth. Add cornstarch mixture and 1 tablespoon freshly grated lemon peel to saucepan. Cook and stir over medium heat 2 minutes or until thickened. Stir in reserved whole cranberries. Remove saucepan from heat. Cool completely.

Streusel Topping: Combine ¾ cup chopped walnuts or pecans, ⅓ cup packed light brown sugar, 2 tablespoons all-purpose flour, ½ teaspoon ground cardamom, ½ teaspoon ground nutmeg and ½ teaspoon ground cinnamon in medium bowl. Stir in 3 tablespoons melted butter until well blended.

Sour Cream Coffee Cake

Orange Streusel Coffeecake

Cocoa Streusel (recipe follows)
¾ cup (1½ sticks) butter or margarine, softened
1 cup sugar
3 eggs
1 teaspoon vanilla extract
½ cup dairy sour cream
3 cups all-purpose flour
2 teaspoons baking powder
1 teaspoon baking soda
1 cup orange juice
2 teaspoons grated orange peel
½ cup orange marmalade or apple jelly

1. Prepare Cocoa Streusel. Heat oven to 350°F. Generously grease 12-cup fluted tube pan.

2. Beat butter and sugar in large bowl until well blended. Add eggs and vanilla; beat well. Add sour cream; beat until blended. Stir together flour, baking powder and baking soda; add alternately with orange juice to butter mixture, beating until well blended. Stir in orange peel.

3. Spread marmalade in bottom of prepared pan; sprinkle half of streusel over marmalade. Pour half of batter into pan, spreading evenly. Sprinkle remaining streusel over batter; spread remaining batter evenly over streusel.

4. Bake about 1 hour or until toothpick inserted near center of cake comes out clean. Loosen cake from side of pan with metal spatula; immediately invert onto serving plate. *Makes 12 servings*

Cocoa Streusel: Stir together ⅔ cup packed light brown sugar, ½ cup chopped walnuts, ¼ cup HERSHEY'S Cocoa and ½ cup MOUNDS® Sweetened Coconut Flakes, if desired.

Orange Streusel Coffeecake

Banana Coffeecake

6 tablespoons margarine, softened
¾ cup sugar
1 egg
1 tablespoon grated lemon peel
1 teaspoon vanilla extract
½ cup milk
2 cups all-purpose flour
1 tablespoon baking powder
¼ teaspoon salt
3 ripe, large DOLE® Bananas, sliced (3 cups)
Streusel Topping (recipe follows)

• Beat margarine and sugar in large bowl until light and fluffy. Beat in egg, lemon peel and vanilla until smooth. Stir in milk.

• Combine flour, baking powder and salt in medium bowl; add to margarine mixture, stirring until blended. Fold in bananas.

• Spoon batter into well greased 9-inch square baking pan; smooth top. Sprinkle with Streusel Topping. Bake at 375°F 45 to 50 minutes until toothpick inserted in center comes out clean. Cool 20 minutes before cutting. *Makes 9 servings*

Streusel Topping: Combine ⅓ cup packed brown sugar, ⅓ cup all-purpose flour and ¾ teaspoon cinnamon. Cut in ¼ cup margarine until mixture is crumbly.

Cinnamon Chip Danish

6 ounces cream cheese, softened
3 tablespoons sugar
1 egg yolk
1⅔ cups (10-ounce package) HERSHEY'S Cinnamon Chips, divided*
10 frozen yeast rolls, thawed and risen
Vanilla Glaze (recipe follows)

REESE'S® Peanut Butter Chips or HERSHEY'S Semi-Sweet Chocolate Chips can be substituted for the cinnamon chips.

1. Beat cream cheese, sugar and egg yolk until well blended. Set aside 3 tablespoons cinnamon chips for garnish. Stir remaining chips into cream cheese mixture.

2. Spray board or counter with nonstick cooking spray. Combine yeast rolls and roll to an 18×12-inch rectangle. Spread filling over center third (lengthwise portion) of rectangle. Cut 1-inch-wide strips from edge of filling to edge of dough along 18-inch sides. Begin braid by folding top row toward filling. Alternately fold strips at an angle from each side across filling toward opposite side. Fold bottom row toward filling and finish by stretching last strip and tucking under.

3. Spray baking sheet with nonstick cooking spray. Support braid with both hands and place diagonally on baking sheet. Cover with sprayed plastic wrap; let rise 25 to 30 minutes. Heat oven to 350°F. Bake 30 minutes or until golden brown. Cool; drizzle with Vanilla Glaze. Garnish with reserved chips.   *Makes about 12 servings*

Vanilla Glaze: Stir together ½ cup powdered sugar, 1½ teaspoons softened butter and enough milk until of desired consistency.

Raspberry Breakfast Braid

Braid
> **2 cups packaged baking mix**
> **1 (3-ounce) package cream cheese**
> **¼ cup butter or margarine**
> **⅓ cup milk**
> **½ cup SMUCKER'S® Red Raspberry Preserves**

Glaze
> **1 cup powdered sugar**
> **¼ teaspoon almond extract**
> **¼ teaspoon vanilla**
> **1 to 2 tablespoons milk**

1. In medium bowl, measure baking mix. Cut in cream cheese and butter until mixture is crumbly. Stir in milk. Turn dough onto lightly floured surface and knead lightly 10 to 12 times. Roll dough into 12×8-inch rectangle. Transfer to greased baking sheet. Spread preserves lengthwise down center ⅓ of dough. Make 2½-inch cuts at 1-inch intervals on long sides. Fold strips over filling.

2. Bake at 425°F for 12 to 15 minutes or until lightly browned.

3. Combine all glaze ingredients, adding enough milk for desired drizzling consistency. Drizzle over coffeecake.   *Makes 10 to 12 servings*

Blueberry Coffeecake

2 cups blueberries, fresh or frozen and partially thawed
1 tablespoon all-purpose flour
½ cup honey
2 tablespoons fresh lemon juice

Cake
1½ cups all-purpose flour
2 teaspoons baking powder
½ teaspoon baking soda
½ teaspoon salt
½ cup honey
2 eggs
¼ cup milk
2 tablespoons fresh lemon juice
1 teaspoon freshly grated lemon peel
1 teaspoon vanilla extract
6 tablespoons butter, melted

Place blueberries in bottom of greased 9-inch round cake pan; distribute evenly. Sprinkle with flour; drizzle with honey and lemon juice. Set aside.

In small bowl, combine flour, baking powder, baking soda and salt; set aside. In medium bowl, combine honey, eggs, milk, lemon juice, lemon peel and vanilla; beat with fork until well mixed. Add flour mixture; mix well. Stir in melted butter; mix well. Pour batter over blueberries in pan; spread to cover evenly. Bake at 350°F for 30 to 35 minutes, or until toothpick inserted in center of cake comes out clean. Cool in pan on wire rack 10 minutes. Invert cake onto large plate; cool.   *Makes 8 servings*

*Favorite recipe from **National Honey Board***

Blueberry Coffeecake

Toll House® Crumbcake

Topping
- ⅓ **cup packed brown sugar**
- 1 **tablespoon all-purpose flour**
- 2 **tablespoons butter or margarine, softened**
- ½ **cup chopped nuts**
- 2 **cups (12-ounce package) NESTLÉ® TOLL HOUSE® Semi-Sweet Chocolate Mini Morsels, *divided***

Cake
- 1¾ **cups all-purpose flour**
- 1 **teaspoon baking powder**
- 1 **teaspoon baking soda**
- ¼ **teaspoon salt**
- ¾ **cup granulated sugar**
- ½ **cup (1 stick) butter or margarine, softened**
- 1 **teaspoon vanilla extract**
- 3 **eggs**
- 1 **cup sour cream**

PREHEAT oven to 350°F. Grease 13×9-inch baking pan.

For Topping

COMBINE brown sugar, flour and butter in small bowl with pastry blender or two knives until crumbly. Stir in nuts and ½ *cup* morsels.

For Cake

COMBINE flour, baking powder, baking soda and salt in small bowl. Beat granulated sugar, butter and vanilla extract in large mixer bowl until creamy. Add eggs, one at a time, beating well after each addition. Gradually add flour mixture alternately with sour cream. Fold in *remaining 1½ cups* morsels. Spread into prepared baking pan; sprinkle with topping.

BAKE for 25 to 35 minutes or until wooden pick inserted in center comes out clean. Cool in pan on wire rack. *Makes 12 servings*

Toll House® Crumbcake

Sun Dried Cherry-Orange Coffee Cake

2 cups all-purpose flour
½ cup granulated sugar
3 teaspoons baking powder
½ teaspoon salt
½ cup CRISCO® Canola Oil
½ cup milk
1 egg, beaten
½ cup chopped sun dried cherries
½ cup fresh orange juice
2 teaspoons grated fresh orange peel
½ cup packed light brown sugar
½ cup chopped pecans
2 tablespoons butter, softened
1 teaspoon ground cinnamon
½ teaspoon ground nutmeg

1. Heat oven to 375°F. Sift together flour, sugar, baking powder and salt in large bowl. Combine oil, milk and egg in small bowl; mix well. Add to flour mixture; stir until blended. Combine cherries, orange juice and orange peel in large bowl; mix well. Add to batter until blended.

2. Spray 9-inch square baking pan with CRISCO® No-Stick Cooking Spray. Dust pan with flour. Pour batter into pan; spread evenly. Combine brown sugar, pecans, butter, cinnamon and nutmeg in large bowl; mix well. Sprinkle over batter.

3. Bake at 375°F for 25 to 30 minutes or until toothpick inserted in center comes out clean. Remove from oven and let cool 5 minutes before serving.

Makes 6 to 8 servings

Sun Dried Cherry-Orange Coffee Cake

Delectable Chocolate Wreath

½ **cup milk**
¼ **cup water (70 to 80°F)**
3 **tablespoons butter or margarine, cut up**
1 **egg**
⅓ **cup sugar**
¼ **cup unsweetened cocoa powder**
¾ **teaspoon salt**
2½ **cups bread or all-purpose flour**
2 **teaspoons FLEISCHMANN'S® Bread Machine Yeast**
   White Chocolate, Raspberry and Pecan Filling (recipe follows)
   Frosting (recipe follows)

Bread Machine Directions

Add all ingredients except filling and frosting to bread machine pan in the order suggested by manufacturer. Select dough/manual cycle. When cycle is complete, remove dough to lightly floured surface. If necessary, knead in enough flour to make dough easy to handle.

Roll dough to 22×6-inch rectangle. With sharp knife, cut in half lengthwise to make two 22×3-inch strips. Spread half of White Chocolate, Raspberry and Pecan Filling down center length of each strip. Fold long sides of dough over filling; pinch seams and ends to seal. Place ropes, seam sides down, on greased large baking sheet. Twist ropes together. Form into wreath; pinch ends to seal. Cover and let rise in warm, draft-free place until risen slightly, about 1 hour.

Bake at 350°F for 35 to 40 minutes or until done. Remove from baking sheet; cool on wire rack. Drizzle with frosting. Garnish with candied fruit, if desired.

Makes 1 wreath

White Chocolate, Raspberry and Pecan Filling: Combine ¾ cup white chocolate morsels, ½ cup chopped toasted pecans and 2 tablespoons seedless red raspberry jam.

Frosting: Combine 1 cup sifted powdered sugar, 1 to 2 tablespoons milk and 1 teaspoon Spice Islands® Pure Vanilla Extract. Stir until smooth.

Delectable Chocolate Wreath

Cherry-Coconut-Cheese Coffee Cake

2½ cups all-purpose flour
¾ cup sugar
½ teaspoon baking powder
½ teaspoon baking soda
2 packages (3 ounces each) cream cheese, softened, divided
¾ cup milk
2 tablespoons vegetable oil
2 eggs, divided
1 teaspoon vanilla
½ cup flaked coconut
¾ cup cherry preserves
2 tablespoons butter

1. Preheat oven to 350°F. Grease and flour 9-inch springform pan. Combine flour and sugar in large bowl. Reserve ½ cup flour mixture. Stir baking powder and baking soda into remaining flour mixture. Cut in 1 package cream cheese with pastry blender or 2 knives until mixture resembles coarse crumbs; set aside.

2. Combine milk, oil and 1 egg in medium bowl. Add to cream cheese mixture; stir just until moistened. Spread batter on bottom and 1 inch up side of prepared pan. Combine remaining package cream cheese, remaining egg and vanilla in small bowl; stir until smooth. Pour over batter, spreading to within 1 inch of edge. Sprinkle coconut over cream cheese mixture. Spoon preserves evenly over coconut.

3. Cut butter into reserved flour mixture with pastry blender or 2 knives until mixture resembles coarse crumbs. Sprinkle over preserves. Bake 55 to 60 minutes or until golden brown and toothpick inserted into crust comes out clean. Cool in pan on wire rack 15 minutes. Remove side of pan; serve warm. *Makes 10 servings*

Cherry-Coconut-Cheese Coffee Cake

Easier Chocolate-Filled Braid

Chocolate Nut Filling (page 104)
2½ to 2¾ cups all-purpose flour, divided
2 tablespoons granulated sugar
½ teaspoon salt
1 package rapid-rise yeast
½ cup milk
¼ cup water
½ cup (1 stick) butter or margarine
1 egg, at room temperature
Vegetable oil
Powdered Sugar Glaze (page 104, optional)

1. Heat oven to 375°F. Grease baking sheet. Prepare Chocolate Nut Filling.

2. Stir together 1½ cups flour, sugar, salt and yeast in large bowl of heavy duty mixer. Combine milk, water and butter in small saucepan; over low heat, heat just until very warm, 125° to 130°F. (Butter might not be melted.) Gradually add to dry ingredients; beat on medium speed of mixer 2 minutes. Add egg and 1 cup flour; beat 2 minutes. Stir in enough remaining flour to form stiff dough. Cover; let rest 10 minutes.

3. Onto well-floured board, turn out dough; roll into 18×10-inch rectangle. Transfer to prepared baking sheet. Spread Chocolate Nut Filling lengthwise down center third of dough. Cut 1-inch-wide strips diagonally on both sides of dough to within ¾ inch of filling. Alternately fold opposite strips of dough at angle across filling. Shape into ring; pinch ends together. Brush lightly with oil; let stand 10 minutes.

4. Bake 20 to 25 minutes or until lightly browned. Remove from baking sheet to wire rack. Cool completely. Prepare Powdered Sugar Glaze, if desired; drizzle over braid.

Makes 10 to 12 servings

continued on page 104

Easier Chocolate-Filled Braid

Easier Chocolate-Filled Braid, continued

Chocolate Nut Filling

¾ cup HERSHEY'S Semi-Sweet Chocolate Chips
2 tablespoons sugar
⅓ cup evaporated milk
½ cup chopped nuts
1 teaspoon vanilla extract
¼ teaspoon ground cinnamon

Stir together chocolate chips, sugar and evaporated milk in small saucepan. Over low heat, cook, stirring constantly, until chips are melted and mixture is smooth. Stir in nuts, vanilla and cinnamon. Cool completely.

Powdered Sugar Glaze

1 cup powdered sugar
1 tablespoon milk
1 teaspoon butter or margarine, softened
½ teaspoon vanilla extract

Stir together powdered sugar, milk, butter and vanilla in small bowl; beat until smooth and of desired consistency. Add additional milk, 1 teaspoon at a time, if needed.

tip

Evaporated milk, not to be confused with sweetened condensed milk, is homogenized milk which has had 60% of its water removed. Sweeteners are not added. Evaporated milk comes in cans and is available made with whole, low-fat and fat-free milk.

Blueberry Sour Cream Tea Ring

Streusel
- ¼ **cup firmly packed brown sugar**
- ¼ **cup chopped pecans**
- ½ **teaspoon ground cinnamon**

Cake
- 1 **package DUNCAN HINES® Bakery-Style Wild Maine Blueberry Muffin Mix**
- ¾ **cup dairy sour cream**
- 1 **egg**
- 2 **tablespoons water**

Glaze
- ½ **cup confectioners' sugar**
- 1 **tablespoon milk**

1. Preheat oven to 350°F. Grease 7-cup tube pan.

2. For streusel, combine brown sugar, pecans and cinnamon in small bowl. Set aside.

3. Rinse blueberries from Mix with cold water and drain.

4. For cake, empty muffin mix into bowl. Break up any lumps. Add sour cream, egg and water. Stir until blended. Pour one-third of batter into pan. Sprinkle half of streusel over batter. Place half of blueberries over streusel. Repeat layers ending with batter on top. Bake at 350°F for 33 to 37 minutes or until toothpick inserted in center comes out clean. Cool in pan 10 minutes. Invert onto cooling rack. Turn right-side-up.

5. For glaze, combine confectioners' sugar and milk in small bowl. Stir until smooth. Drizzle over warm cake. *Makes 12 servings*

Apple Crumb Coffeecake

2¼ cups all-purpose flour
½ cup sugar
1 envelope FLEISCHMANN'S® RapidRise™ Yeast
½ teaspoon salt
¼ cup water
¼ cup milk
⅓ cup butter or margarine
2 eggs
2 cooking apples, cored and sliced
Crumb Topping (recipe follows)

In large bowl, combine 1 cup flour, sugar, undissolved yeast, and salt. Heat water, milk and butter until very warm (120° to 130°F). Gradually add to dry ingredients. Beat 2 minutes at medium speed of electric mixer, scraping bowl occasionally. Add eggs and ½ cup flour. Beat 2 minutes at high speed, scraping bowl occasionally. Stir in remaining flour to make stiff batter. Spread evenly in greased 9-inch square pan. Arrange apple slices evenly over batter. Sprinkle Crumb Topping over apples. Cover; let rise in warm, draft-free place until doubled in size, about 1 hour.

Bake at 375°F for 35 to 40 minutes or until done. Cool in pan 10 minutes. Remove from pan; cool on wire rack. *Makes 1 (9-inch) cake*

Crumb Topping: Combine ⅓ cup sugar, ¼ cup all-purpose flour, 1 teaspoon ground cinnamon, and 3 tablespoons cold butter or margarine. Mix until crumbly.

Note: For best results use a pastry blender to cut into the cold butter or margarine. Mix all ingredients until coarse crumbs form.

Apple Crumb Coffeecake

delicious quick breads

Rich Cranberry Scones

    3 cups all-purpose flour
⅓ cup plus 1 tablespoon sugar, divided
1 tablespoon baking powder
½ teaspoon salt
6 tablespoons I CAN'T BELIEVE IT'S NOT BUTTER!® Spread
¾ cup dried cranberries
1 cup plus 1 tablespoon whipping or heavy cream, divided
2 eggs

Preheat oven to 450°F.

In large bowl, combine flour, ⅓ cup sugar, baking powder and salt. With pastry blender or 2 knives, cut in I Can't Believe It's Not Butter!® Spread until mixture is size of fine crumbs. Stir in cranberries.

In small bowl, with wire whisk, blend 1 cup cream and eggs. Stir into flour mixture until dough forms. On floured surface, with floured hands, divide dough in half. Press each half into 6-inch circle. Cut each circle into 6 pie-shaped wedges. On baking sheet, arrange wedges. Brush with remaining 1 tablespoon cream, then sprinkle with remaining 1 tablespoon sugar.

Bake 12 minutes or until golden. Serve warm or cool completely on wire rack.

Makes 12 scones

Rich Cranberry Scones

Peanut Butter Chocolate Chip Loaves

        3 cups all-purpose flour
    1½ teaspoons baking powder
        1 teaspoon baking soda
        1 teaspoon salt
        1 cup creamy peanut butter
     ½ cup granulated sugar
     ½ cup packed light brown sugar
     ½ cup (1 stick) butter, softened
        2 eggs
    1½ cups buttermilk*
        2 teaspoons vanilla
        1 cup miniature semisweet chocolate chips

Soured fresh milk can be substituted for buttermilk. To sour milk, combine 4½ teaspoons lemon juice plus enough milk to equal 1½ cups. Stir; let stand 5 minutes before using.

1. Preheat oven to 350°F. Spray two 8½×4½-inch loaf pans with nonstick cooking spray; set aside.

2. Sift flour, baking powder, baking soda and salt into large bowl. Beat peanut butter, granulated sugar, brown sugar and butter in another large bowl with electric mixer at medium speed until light and fluffy. Beat in eggs, one at a time. Beat in buttermilk and vanilla. Gradually add flour mixture. Beat at low speed until blended. Stir in chocolate chips. Divide batter evenly between prepared pans.

3. Bake 45 minutes or until toothpicks inserted into centers come out clean. Cool in pans on wire racks 10 minutes. Remove from pans and cool completely on wire racks.   *Makes 24 servings*

Variation: Stir in ¾ cup chocolate chips before baking; sprinkle with remaining ¼ cup after baking.

Peanut Butter Chocolate Chip Loaf

Honey Sweet Potato Biscuits

      2 cups all-purpose flour
      1 tablespoon baking powder
  ½ teaspoon salt
  ¼ cup vegetable shortening
      1 tablespoon grated orange peel
      1 tablespoon grated lemon peel
  ¾ cup mashed cooked sweet potato (1 large sweet potato baked
          until tender, peeled and mashed)
  ⅓ cup honey
  ½ cup milk (about)

Combine flour, baking powder and salt in large bowl. Cut in shortening until mixture is size of small peas. Add orange and lemon peels, sweet potato and honey; mix well. Add enough milk to make soft, but not sticky, dough. Knead 3 or 4 times on lightly floured surface. Pat dough to 1-inch thickness and cut into 2¼-inch rounds. Place on ungreased baking sheet.

Bake in preheated 400°F oven 15 to 18 minutes or until lightly browned. Serve warm.

Makes 10 biscuits

*Favorite recipe from **National Honey Board***

Old-Fashioned Corn Bread

      1 cup sifted all-purpose flour
  ¾ teaspoon ARM & HAMMER® Baking Soda
      1 teaspoon salt
  1½ cups cornmeal
      2 eggs, beaten
  1½ cups buttermilk
      3 tablespoons shortening, melted

Sift together flour, Baking Soda, and salt. Stir in cornmeal. Combine eggs, buttermilk and melted shortening. Add liquid ingredients to dry ingredients, stirring only until smooth. Turn into well-greased 8×8-inch pan. Bake at 425°F 20 to 25 minutes.

Makes 16 servings

Honey Sweet Potato Biscuits

Banana Nut Bread

½ cup granulated sugar
2 tablespoons brown sugar
5 tablespoons margarine
1⅓ cups mashed ripe bananas (2 medium)
1 egg
2 egg whites
2½ cups all-purpose flour
1 teaspoon baking soda
½ teaspoon salt
⅓ cup walnuts

Preheat oven to 375°F. Spray large loaf pan with nonstick cooking spray; set aside.

Beat sugars and margarine in large bowl with electric mixer until light and fluffy. Add bananas, egg and egg whites. Sift together flour, baking soda and salt in medium bowl; add to banana mixture. Stir in walnuts. Pour into prepared loaf pan.

Bake 1 hour or until wooden pick inserted in center comes out clean. Remove from pan. Cool on wire rack 10 minutes. Serve warm or cool completely.

Makes 1 loaf (16 servings)

Favorite recipe from **The Sugar Association, Inc.**

Baking Powder Biscuits

2¼ cups all-purpose flour
1 tablespoon baking powder
½ teaspoon salt
¼ cup (½ stick) cold butter, cut into 4 pieces
¾ cup milk

Preheat oven to 450°F. Fit food processor with steel blade. Place flour, baking powder and salt in work bowl. Process on/off to mix. Add butter; process until mixture resembles coarse crumbs, about 10 seconds. Pour milk over flour mixture. Process on/off 6 to 8 times, or just until flour is blended in and dough is soft. Turn out dough onto lightly floured surface. Knead gently 6 to 8 times. Roll or pat dough out until ½ inch thick. Cut dough into 2½-inch circles using floured cutter. Place biscuits on ungreased baking sheet. Bake 12 to 15 minutes or until golden. *Makes 1 dozen biscuits*

Banana Nut Bread

Irish Soda Bread

4 cups all-purpose flour
¼ cup sugar
1 tablespoon baking powder
1 teaspoon baking soda
1 teaspoon salt
1 tablespoon caraway seeds
⅓ cup shortening
1 cup raisins or currants
1 egg
1¾ cups buttermilk*

*Soured fresh milk can be substituted for buttermilk. To sour milk, combine 2 tablespoons lemon juice plus enough milk to equal 1¾ cups. Stir; let stand 5 minutes before using.

1. Preheat oven to 350°F. Grease large baking sheet; set aside.

2. Sift flour, sugar, baking powder, baking soda and salt into large bowl. Stir in caraway seeds. Cut in shortening with pastry blender or 2 knives until mixture resembles coarse crumbs. Stir in raisins. Beat egg in medium bowl. Add buttermilk; beat until well blended. Add buttermilk mixture to flour mixture; stir until mixture forms soft dough that clings together and forms a ball.

3. Turn out dough onto well-floured surface. Knead dough gently 10 to 12 times. Place dough on prepared baking sheet. Pat dough into 7-inch round. Score top of dough with tip of sharp knife, making an "X" about 4 inches long and ¼ inch deep.

4. Bake 55 to 60 minutes or until toothpick inserted into center comes out clean. Immediately remove from baking sheet; cool on wire rack.** Bread is best eaten the day it is made. *Makes 12 servings*

**For a sweet crust, combine 1 tablespoon sugar and 1 tablespoon water in small bowl; brush over hot loaf.

Irish Soda Bread

Apricot Carrot Bread

1¾ cups all-purpose flour
1 teaspoon baking powder
¼ teaspoon baking soda
¼ teaspoon salt
½ cup granulated sugar
½ cup finely shredded carrots
½ cup MOTT'S® Natural Apple Sauce
1 egg, beaten lightly
2 tablespoons vegetable oil
⅓ cup dried apricots, snipped into small bits
½ cup powdered sugar
2 teaspoons MOTT'S® Apple Juice

1. Preheat oven to 350°F. Spray 8×4-inch loaf pan with nonstick cooking spray.

2. In large bowl, combine flour, baking powder, baking soda and salt.

3. In small bowl, combine granulated sugar, carrots, apple sauce, egg and oil.

4. Stir apple sauce mixture into flour mixture just until moistened. (Batter will be thick.) Fold in apricots. Spread batter in prepared pan.

5. Bake 45 to 50 minutes or until toothpick inserted in center comes out clean. Cool in pan 10 minutes. Invert onto wire rack; turn right side up. Cool completely. For best flavor, wrap loaf in plastic wrap or foil; store at room temperature overnight.

6. Just before serving, in small bowl, combine powdered sugar and apple juice until smooth. Drizzle over top of loaf. Cut into 12 slices.   *Makes 12 servings*

Apricot Carrot Bread

Onion-Zucchini Bread

    1 large zucchini (¾ pound), shredded
2½ cups all-purpose flour*
1⅓ cups *French's*® French Fried Onions
    ⅓ cup grated Parmesan cheese
    1 tablespoon baking powder
    1 tablespoon chopped fresh basil or 1 teaspoon dried basil leaves
    ½ teaspoon salt
    ¾ cup milk
    ½ cup (1 stick) butter or margarine, melted
    ¼ cup packed light brown sugar
    2 eggs

You can substitute 1¼ cups whole wheat flour for 1¼ cups all-purpose flour.

1. Preheat oven to 350°F. Grease 9×5×3-inch loaf pan.

2. Drain zucchini in colander. Combine flour, French Fried Onions, cheese, baking powder, basil and salt in large bowl.

3. Combine milk, butter, brown sugar and eggs in medium bowl; whisk until well blended. Place zucchini in kitchen towel; squeeze out excess liquid. Stir zucchini into milk mixture.

4. Stir milk mixture into flour mixture, stirring just until moistened. Do not overmix. (Batter will be very stiff and dry.) Spread batter in prepared pan. Run knife down center of batter.

5. Bake 50 to 65 minutes or until toothpick inserted in center comes out clean. Cool in pan on wire rack 10 minutes. Remove bread from pan to wire rack; cool completely. Cut into slices to serve.**   *Makes 10 to 12 servings*

**For optimum flavor, wrap bread overnight and serve the next day. Great when toasted!*

Prep Time: 20 minutes
Bake Time: about 1 hour

Onion-Zucchini Bread

Tex-Mex Quick Bread

1½ cups all-purpose flour
1 cup (4 ounces) shredded Monterey Jack cheese
½ cup cornmeal
½ cup sun-dried tomatoes, coarsely chopped
1 can (about 4 ounces) black olives, drained and chopped
¼ cup sugar
1½ teaspoons baking powder
1 teaspoon baking soda
1 cup milk
1 can (about 4 ounces) green chilies, drained and chopped
¼ cup olive oil
1 egg, beaten

1. Preheat oven to 325°F. Grease 9×5-inch loaf pan or four 5×3-inch loaf pans; set aside.

2. Combine flour, cheese, cornmeal, tomatoes, olives, sugar, baking powder and baking soda in large bowl.

3. Combine remaining ingredients in small bowl. Add to flour mixture; stir just until blended. Pour into prepared pan. Bake 9×5-inch loaf 45 minutes and 5×3-inch loaves 30 minutes or until toothpick inserted near center of loaf comes out clean. Cool in pan 15 minutes. Remove from pan and cool on wire rack.

Makes 1 large loaf or 4 small loaves

tip

Sun-dried tomatoes are tomatoes that have been naturally or artificially dried. They can be purchased either packed in oil in jars or packaged dry in cellophane. The oil-packed variety tends to be more expensive, but once drained, is ready to use. The dry variety needs to be softened before using. To soften dry sun-dried tomatoes, cover them with hot water for 30 minutes or boiling water for 5 minutes and then drain well.

Tex-Mex Quick Bread

Italian Herb Biscuit Loaf

1½ **cups all-purpose flour**
¼ **cup grated Parmesan cheese**
2 **tablespoons cornmeal**
2 **teaspoons baking powder**
½ **teaspoon salt**
¼ **cup (½ stick) butter**
2 **eggs**
½ **cup whipping cream**
¾ **teaspoon dried basil leaves**
¾ **teaspoon dried oregano leaves**
⅛ **teaspoon garlic powder**
Additional Parmesan cheese (optional)

1. Preheat oven to 425°F. Spray large baking sheet with nonstick cooking spray; set aside.

2. Combine flour, ¼ cup cheese, cornmeal, baking powder and salt in large bowl. Cut in butter with pastry blender or 2 knives until mixture resembles coarse crumbs. Beat eggs in medium bowl. Add cream, basil, oregano and garlic powder; beat until well blended. Add cream mixture to flour mixture; stir until mixture forms ball.

3. Turn out dough onto well-floured surface. Knead 10 to 12 times; place on prepared baking sheet. Roll or pat dough into 7-inch round, about 1 inch thick. Score top of dough into 8 wedges with tip of sharp knife; do not cut completely through dough. Sprinkle with additional cheese, if desired.

4. Bake 20 to 25 minutes or until toothpick inserted into center comes out clean. Cool on baking sheet on wire rack 10 minutes. Serve warm. *Makes 8 servings*

Italian Herb Biscuit Loaf

Walnut-Chocolate Quick Bread

1½ cups milk
1 cup sugar
⅓ cup vegetable oil
1 egg, beaten
1 tablespoon molasses
1 teaspoon vanilla
3 cups all-purpose flour
3 tablespoons unsweetened cocoa powder
2 teaspoons baking soda
2 teaspoons baking powder
1 teaspoon salt
1 cup chocolate chips
½ cup walnuts, coarsely chopped

1. Preheat oven to 350°F. Grease four 5×3-inch loaf pans; set aside.

2. Combine milk, sugar, oil, egg, molasses and vanilla in medium bowl. Stir until sugar is dissolved.

3. Combine flour, cocoa, baking soda, baking powder and salt in large bowl. Add chocolate chips, walnuts and milk mixture; stir just until combined. Pour into prepared pans.

4. Bake 30 minutes or until toothpicks inserted into centers of loaves come out clean. Cool in pans 15 minutes. Remove from pans and cool on wire racks.

Makes 4 small loaves

Walnut-Chocolate Quick Bread

Chive Whole Wheat Drop Biscuits

1¼ cups whole wheat flour
¾ cup all-purpose flour
3 tablespoons toasted wheat germ, divided
1 tablespoon baking powder
1 tablespoon chopped fresh chives *or* **1 teaspoon dried chives**
2 teaspoons sugar
3 tablespoons cold butter
1 cup fat-free (skim) milk
½ cup shredded Cheddar cheese

Preheat oven to 450°F. Lightly grease baking sheet. Mix flours, 2 tablespoons wheat germ, baking powder, chives and sugar in large bowl. Cut in butter with pastry blender until mixture resembles coarse meal. Add milk and cheese; stir until just blended. Drop dough by rounded tablespoonfuls about 1 inch apart onto prepared baking sheet. Sprinkle with remaining 1 tablespoon wheat germ. Bake 10 to 12 minutes or until golden. Transfer to wire rack to cool slightly. *Makes 12 servings*

Hot Pepper Cheddar Loaf

2½ cups flour
1 tablespoon baking powder
½ teaspoon salt
¼ teaspoon fresh ground black pepper
2 eggs
1 cup skim milk
1 tablespoon vegetable oil
2 teaspoons TABASCO® brand Pepper Sauce
8 ounces shredded sharp Cheddar cheese
1 teaspoon chopped jalapeño pepper (optional)

Preheat oven to 350°F. Grease 9×5-inch loaf pan.

Combine flour, baking powder, salt, and pepper in large bowl. Combine eggs, milk, oil, and TABASCO® Sauce in medium bowl. Add egg mixture to dry ingredients just until blended. Stir in cheese and jalapeño pepper.

Spoon batter into prepared pan and place on rack in center of oven. Bake 45 to 50 minutes until lightly browned and firm. *Makes 1 loaf (10 servings)*

Chive Whole Wheat Drop Biscuits

Aloha Bread

1 (10-ounce) jar maraschino cherries
1¾ cups all-purpose flour
2 teaspoons baking powder
½ teaspoon salt
⅔ cup firmly packed brown sugar
⅓ cup butter or margarine, softened
2 eggs
1 cup mashed ripe bananas
½ cup chopped macadamia nuts or walnuts

Drain maraschino cherries, reserving 2 tablespoons juice. Cut cherries into quarters; set aside.

Combine flour, baking powder and salt in small bowl; set aside.

In medium bowl, combine brown sugar, butter, eggs and reserved cherry juice; mix on medium speed of electric mixer until ingredients are thoroughly blended. Add flour mixture alternately with mashed bananas, beginning and ending with flour mixture. Stir in cherries and nuts. Lightly spray 9×5×3-inch loaf pan with nonstick cooking spray. Spread batter evenly in pan.

Bake in preheated 350°F oven 1 hour or until loaf is golden brown and wooden pick inserted near center comes out clean. Remove from pan and cool on wire rack. Store in tightly covered container or foil. *Makes 1 loaf (about 16 slices)*

Favorite recipe from **Cherry Marketing Institute**

tip

Quick breads require very little mixing and no rising time prior to baking. Bake these breads immediately after they are mixed so that leaveners do not lose their power. For quick-batter breads, such as muffins and tea breads, the batter should look lumpy when it goes into the prepared pan. Too much stirring or beating will give the breads a tough texture with lots of holes and tunnels.

Aloha Bread

Cranberry Oat Bread

¾ **cup honey**
⅓ **cup vegetable oil**
 2 **eggs**
½ **cup milk**
2½ **cups all-purpose flour**
 1 **cup quick-cooking rolled oats**
 1 **teaspoon baking soda**
 1 **teaspoon baking powder**
½ **teaspoon salt**
½ **teaspoon ground cinnamon**
 2 **cups fresh or frozen cranberries**
 1 **cup chopped nuts**

Combine honey, oil, eggs and milk in large bowl; mix well. Combine flour, oats, baking soda, baking powder, salt and cinnamon in medium bowl; mix well. Stir into honey mixture. Fold in cranberries and nuts. Spoon into 2 greased and floured 8½×4½×2½-inch loaf pans.

Bake in preheated 350°F oven 40 to 45 minutes or until wooden toothpick inserted near centers comes out clean. Cool in pans on wire racks 15 minutes. Remove from pans; cool completely on wire racks. *Makes 2 loaves*

Favorite recipe from **National Honey Board**

Cranberry Oat Bread

Cheddar-Apple Bread

     2 cups all-purpose flour
     2 teaspoons baking powder
     1 teaspoon baking soda
     ¼ teaspoon salt
     1 cup sour cream
     ¼ cup milk
     1 cup packed light brown sugar
     ½ cup (1 stick) butter, softened
     2 eggs
     1 teaspoon vanilla
   1½ cups diced dried apples
     1 cup (4 ounces) shredded Cheddar cheese

1. Preheat oven to 350°F. Spray 9×5-inch loaf pan with nonstick cooking spray; set aside.

2. Combine flour, baking powder, baking soda and salt in small bowl. Combine sour cream and milk in another small bowl. Beat brown sugar and butter in large bowl with electric mixer at medium speed until light and fluffy. Beat in eggs and vanilla until blended. Add flour mixture to butter mixture alternately with sour cream mixture, beginning and ending with flour mixture. Beat well after each addition. Stir in apples and cheese until blended. Spoon into prepared pan.

3. Bake 50 to 55 minutes or until toothpick inserted into center comes out clean. Cool in pan on wire rack 15 minutes. Remove from pan and cool completely on wire rack. *Makes 12 servings*

Hint: Brown sugar can become hard during storage, making it difficult to measure. To soften it, place the brown sugar in a microwavable bowl and microwave at HIGH 30 to 60 seconds or until softened.

Cheddar-Apple Bread

Chocolate-Raspberry Loaf

 1 cup semisweet chocolate chips
¼ cup (½ stick) butter
 2 cups all-purpose flour
½ cup sugar
 1 teaspoon baking soda
½ teaspoon baking powder
¼ teaspoon salt
 1 cup toasted finely chopped walnuts
 2 eggs
¾ cup milk
½ cup seedless raspberry spreadable fruit
 1 teaspoon vanilla

1. Preheat oven to 350°F. Spray 9×5-inch loaf pan with nonstick cooking spray; set aside. Melt chocolate chips and butter in small saucepan over low heat.

2. Combine flour, sugar, baking soda, baking powder and salt in large bowl. Add walnuts; mix well. Lightly beat eggs in medium bowl with wire whisk. Add milk, spreadable fruit and vanilla; beat until well blended. Add chocolate and milk mixtures to flour mixture. Stir just until moistened. Spread in prepared pan.

3. Bake 50 to 60 minutes or until toothpick inserted into center comes out clean. Cool in pan on wire rack 10 minutes. Remove from pan and cool completely on wire rack. *Makes 12 servings*

tip

Always measure baking powder and baking soda carefully. Too much leavening gives a quick bread a dry texture and a bitter aftertaste. It can even cause the bread to rise too much and fall. Too little leavening produces bread with a dense, heavy texture.

Chocolate-Raspberry Loaf

Date Nut Bread

   2 cups all-purpose flour
  ½ cup packed light brown sugar
   1 tablespoon baking powder
  ½ teaspoon salt
  ¼ cup (½ stick) cold butter
   1 cup *each* toasted chopped walnuts and chopped dates
1 ¼ cups milk
   1 egg
  ½ teaspoon grated lemon peel

Preheat oven to 375°F. Lightly grease 9×5-inch loaf pan; set aside. Combine flour, brown sugar, baking powder and salt in large bowl. Cut in butter with pastry blender or 2 knives until mixture resembles fine crumbs. Add walnuts and dates; stir until coated. Beat milk, egg and lemon peel in small bowl with fork. Add to flour mixture; stir just until moistened. Spread in prepared pan. Bake 45 to 50 minutes or until toothpick inserted into center comes out clean. Cool in pan on wire rack 10 minutes. Remove from pan; cool completely on wire rack.   *Makes 12 servings*

Cheese Scones

1 ½ cups *each* all-purpose flour and uncooked quick-cooking oats
  ¼ cup packed brown sugar
   1 tablespoon baking powder
   1 teaspoon cream of tartar
  ½ teaspoon salt
  ½ cup (2 ounces) finely shredded Cheddar cheese
  ⅔ cup butter, melted
  ⅓ cup milk
   1 egg

Preheat oven to 425°F. Stir together flour, oats, brown sugar, baking powder, cream of tartar and salt in large bowl. Stir in cheese. Beat together butter, milk and egg in small bowl. Add to dry ingredients, stirring just until mixed. Shape dough into ball; pat onto lightly floured surface to form 8-inch circle. Cut into 8 to 12 wedges. Bake on buttered baking sheet 12 to 15 minutes until light golden brown.   *Makes 8 to 12 scones*

*Favorite recipe from **Wisconsin Milk Marketing Board***

Date Nut Bread

Zesty Parmesan Biscuits

4 cups all-purpose flour
½ cup grated Parmesan cheese
2 tablespoons baking powder
2 teaspoons sugar
1 teaspoon baking soda
6 tablespoons cold butter, cut into pieces
6 tablespoons cold solid vegetable shortening
1 cup plus 2 tablespoons buttermilk, divided
½ cup *Frank's® RedHot®* Original Cayenne Pepper Sauce
Sesame seeds (optional)

1. Preheat oven to 450°F. Place flour, cheese, baking powder, sugar and baking soda in food processor or blender.* Cover; process 30 seconds. Add butter and shortening; process, pulsing on and off, until fine crumbs form. Transfer to large bowl.

2. Add 1 cup buttermilk and **Frank's RedHot** Sauce all at once. Stir together just until mixture starts to form a ball. (Dough will be dry. Do not over mix.)

3. Turn dough out onto lightly floured board. With palms of hands, gently knead 8 times. Using floured rolling pin or hands, roll dough to ¾-inch thickness. Using 2½-inch round biscuit cutter, cut out 16 biscuits, re-rolling dough as necessary.

4. Place biscuits 2 inches apart on large foil-lined baking sheet. Brush tops with remaining 2 tablespoons buttermilk; sprinkle with sesame seeds, if desired. Bake 12 to 15 minutes or until golden. *Makes 16 biscuits*

Or, place dry ingredients in large bowl. Cut in butter and shortening until fine crumbs form using pastry blender or 2 knives. Add buttermilk and Frank's RedHot Sauce; mix just until moistened. Continue with step 3.

Prep Time: 30 minutes
Bake Time: 12 minutes

Zesty Parmesan Biscuits

tasty muffins & cupcakes

Blueberry White Chip Muffins

> **2 cups all-purpose flour**
> **½ cup granulated sugar**
> **¼ cup packed brown sugar**
> **2½ teaspoons baking powder**
> **½ teaspoon salt**
> **¾ cup milk**
> **1 egg, lightly beaten**
> **¼ cup butter or margarine, melted**
> **½ teaspoon grated lemon peel**
> **2 cups (12-ounce package) NESTLÉ® TOLL HOUSE® Premier White Morsels, *divided***
> **1½ cups fresh or frozen blueberries**
> **Streusel Topping (recipe follows)**

PREHEAT oven to 375°F. Paper-line 18 muffin cups.

COMBINE flour, granulated sugar, brown sugar, baking powder and salt in large bowl. Stir in milk, egg, butter and lemon peel. Stir in *1½ cups* morsels and blueberries. Spoon into prepared muffin cups, filling almost full. Sprinkle with Streusel Topping.

BAKE for 22 to 25 minutes or until wooden pick inserted in center comes out clean. Cool in pans for 5 minutes; remove to wire racks to cool slightly.

PLACE *remaining* morsels in small, *heavy-duty* resealable plastic food storage bag. Microwave on MEDIUM–HIGH (70%) power for 30 seconds; knead. Microwave at additional 10- to 15-second intervals, kneading until smooth. Cut tiny corner from bag; squeeze to drizzle over muffins. Serve warm. *Makes 18 muffins*

Streusel Topping: COMBINE ⅓ cup granulated sugar, ¼ cup all-purpose flour and ¼ teaspoon ground cinnamon in small bowl. Cut in 3 tablespoons butter or margarine with pastry blender or two knives until mixture resembles coarse crumbs.

Blueberry White Chip Muffins

Fudgey Chocolate Cupcakes

    ¾ cup water
    ½ cup (1 stick) 60% vegetable oil spread, melted
    2 egg whites, slightly beaten
    1 teaspoon vanilla extract
  2¼ cups HERSHEY'S Basic Cocoa Baking Mix (recipe follows)
    2 teaspoons powdered sugar
    2 teaspoons HERSHEY'S Cocoa (optional)

1. Heat oven to 350°F. Line 16 muffin cups (2½ inches in diameter) with foil or paper baking cups.

2. Stir together water, melted spread, egg whites and vanilla in large bowl. Add Basic Cocoa Baking Mix; beat on low speed of mixer until blended. Fill muffin cups ⅔ full with batter.

3. Bake 20 to 25 minutes or until wooden pick inserted into centers comes out clean. Remove from pans to wire racks. Cool completely. Sift powdered sugar over tops of cupcakes. If desired, partially cover part of each cupcake with paper cutout. Sift cocoa over exposed powdered sugar. Carefully lift off cutout. Store, covered, at room temperature.   *Makes 16 cupcakes*

Hershey's Basic Cocoa Baking Mix: Stir together 4½ cups all-purpose flour, 2¾ cups sugar, 1¼ cups HERSHEY'S Cocoa, 1 tablespoon plus ½ teaspoon baking powder, 1¾ teaspoons salt and 1¼ teaspoons baking soda. Store in airtight container in cool, dry place for up to 1 month. Stir before using. Makes 8 cups mix.

Fudgey Chocolate Cupcakes

Cranberry Brunch Muffins

1 cup chopped fresh cranberries
⅓ cup plus ¼ cup sugar, divided
2 cups all-purpose flour
2 teaspoons baking powder
¾ teaspoon salt
½ cup (1 stick) butter
¾ cup orange juice
1 egg, lightly beaten
1 teaspoon vanilla
2 tablespoons butter, melted

1. Preheat oven to 400°F. Lightly grease 12 standard (2½-inch) muffin pan cups or line with paper baking cups.

2. Combine cranberries and 1 tablespoon sugar in small bowl. Blend flour, ⅓ cup sugar, baking powder and salt in large bowl. Cut in ½ cup butter until mixture is crumbly. Stir in orange juice, egg and vanilla just until ingredients are moistened. Fold in cranberry mixture; spoon batter into prepared pan.

3. Bake 20 to 25 minutes or until golden. Cool 5 minutes before removing from pan. Dip tops of muffins in melted butter; sprinkle with remaining 3 tablespoons sugar. Serve warm. *Makes 12 muffins*

tip

Fresh cranberries are readily available September through December. Since they are not available fresh other months of the year, buy an extra bag or two for the freezer. Fresh unwashed cranberries can be kept in an unopened plastic bag for up to one month in the refrigerator and for up to one year in the freezer. Double wrap the bag with freezer wrap before freezing.

Cranberry Brunch Muffins

Cookies & Cream Cupcakes

2¼ cups all-purpose flour
1 tablespoon baking powder
½ teaspoon salt
1⅔ cups sugar
1 cup milk
½ cup (1 stick) butter, softened
2 teaspoons vanilla
3 egg whites
1 cup crushed chocolate sandwich cookies (about 10 cookies) plus additional for garnish
1 container (16 ounces) vanilla frosting

1. Preheat oven to 350°F. Lightly grease 24 standard (2½-inch) muffin pan cups or line with paper baking cups.

2. Sift flour, baking powder and salt together in large bowl. Stir in sugar. Add milk, butter and vanilla; beat with electric mixer at low speed 30 seconds. Beat at medium speed 2 minutes. Add egg whites; beat 2 minutes. Stir in 1 cup crushed cookies.

3. Spoon batter evenly into prepared muffin cups. Bake 20 to 25 minutes or until toothpicks inserted into centers come out clean. Cool in pans on wire racks about 10 minutes. Remove to wire racks; cool completely.

4. Frost cupcakes; garnish with additional crushed cookies.   *Makes 24 cupcakes*

Cookies & Cream Cupcakes

Southern Biscuit Muffins

2½ cups all-purpose flour
¼ cup sugar
1½ tablespoons baking powder
¾ cup (1½ sticks) cold butter
1 cup cold milk
Jelly, jam or honey (optional)

Preheat oven to 400°F. Grease 12 standard (2½-inch) muffin pan cups. (These muffins brown better on the sides and bottoms when baked without paper liners.) Combine flour, sugar and baking powder in large bowl. Cut in butter with pastry blender until mixture resembles coarse crumbs. Stir in milk just until flour mixture is moistened. Spoon evenly into prepared muffin cups. Bake 20 minutes or until golden. Remove from pan. Cool on wire rack. Serve with jelly, jam or honey, if desired.

Makes 12 muffins

Bacon-Cheese Muffins

½ pound bacon (10 to 12 slices)
Vegetable oil
1 egg, beaten
¾ cup milk
1¾ cups all-purpose flour
¼ cup sugar
1 tablespoon baking powder
1 cup (4 ounces) shredded Wisconsin Cheddar cheese
½ cup crunchy nutlike cereal nuggets

Preheat oven to 400°F. In large skillet, cook bacon over medium-high heat until crisp. Drain, reserving drippings. If necessary, add oil to drippings to measure ⅓ cup. In small bowl, combine dripping mixture, egg and milk; set aside. Crumble bacon; set aside.

In large bowl, combine flour, sugar and baking powder. Make well in center. Add egg mixture all at once to flour mixture, stirring just until moistened. Batter should be lumpy. Fold in bacon, cheese and cereal. Spoon into greased or paper-lined 2½-inch muffin cups, filling about ¾ full. Bake 15 to 20 minutes or until golden. Remove from pan. Cool on wire rack.

Makes 12 muffins

Favorite recipe from **Wisconsin Milk Marketing Board**

Bacon-Cheese Muffins

Peanut Butter Surprise

2 cups all-purpose flour
2 teaspoons baking powder
¼ teaspoon salt
1¾ cups sugar
½ cup (1 stick) butter, softened
¾ cup milk
1 teaspoon vanilla
3 egg whites
2 bars (3 ounces each) bittersweet chocolate candy, melted and cooled
30 mini peanut butter cups
1 container prepared chocolate frosting
3 squares (1 ounce each) white chocolate, chopped

1. Preheat oven to 350°F. Lightly grease 30 standard (2½-inch) muffin pan cups or line with paper baking cups.

2. For cupcakes, combine flour, baking powder and salt in medium bowl; mix well. Set aside. Beat sugar and butter in large bowl with electric mixer at medium speed 1 minute. Add milk and vanilla. Beat at low speed 30 seconds. Gradually beat in flour mixture; beat at medium speed 2 minutes. Add egg whites; beat 1 minute. Stir in melted chocolate.

3. Spoon 1 heaping tablespoon batter into each prepared muffin cup; use back of spoon to spread batter over bottom. Place 1 mini peanut butter cup in center of each cupcake. Spoon 1 heaping tablespoon batter over peanut butter cup; use back of spoon to smooth out batter. (Do not fill cups more than ¾ full.)

4. Bake 24 to 26 minutes or until puffed and browned at edges. Cool in pans on wire racks 10 minutes. (Centers of cupcakes will sink slightly upon cooling.) Remove to wire racks; cool completely. Frost cooled cupcakes.

5. For white drizzle, place white chocolate in small resealable plastic food storage bag. Microwave at HIGH 30 to 40 seconds. Turn bag over; microwave additional 30 seconds or until white chocolate is melted. Cut off tiny corner of bag; pipe white chocolate decoratively over frosted cupcakes. *Makes 30 cupcakes*

Peanut Butter Surprise

Chunky Apple Molasses Muffins

    2 cups all-purpose flour
¼ cup sugar
    1 tablespoon baking powder
    1 teaspoon ground cinnamon
¼ teaspoon salt
    1 Fuji apple, peeled, cored and finely chopped
½ cup milk
¼ cup vegetable oil
¼ cup molasses
    1 egg

1. Heat oven to 450°F. Lightly grease eight 3-inch muffin pan cups. In large bowl, combine flour, sugar, baking powder, cinnamon and salt. Add apple and stir to distribute evenly.

2. In small bowl, beat together milk, oil, molasses and egg. Stir into dry ingredients and mix just until blended. Fill muffin pan cups with batter. Bake 5 minutes. Reduce heat to 350°F; bake 12 to 15 minutes longer or until centers of muffins spring back when gently pressed. Cool in pan 5 minutes. Remove muffins from pan and cool slightly; serve warm.   *Makes 8 (3-inch) muffins*

Favorite recipe from **Washington Apple Commission**

tip

An apple corer is an inexpensive utensil that removes the core of an apple while leaving the apple whole. An apple corer/slicer is a wheel-shaped utensil that not only removes the core of an apple or pear but also cuts it into wedges.

Chunky Apple Molasses Muffins

Fudgey Peanut Butter Chip Muffins

½ cup applesauce
½ cup quick-cooking rolled oats
¼ cup (½ stick) butter or margarine, softened
½ cup granulated sugar
½ cup packed light brown sugar
1 egg
½ teaspoon vanilla extract
¾ cup all-purpose flour
¼ cup HERSHEY'S Dutch Processed Cocoa or HERSHEY'S Cocoa
½ teaspoon baking soda
¼ teaspoon ground cinnamon (optional)
1 cup REESE'S® Peanut Butter Chips
Powdered sugar (optional)

1. Heat oven to 350°F. Line muffin cups (2½ inches in diameter) with paper baking cups.

2. Stir together applesauce and oats in small bowl; set aside. Beat butter, granulated sugar, brown sugar, egg and vanilla in large bowl until well blended. Add applesauce mixture; blend well. Stir together flour, cocoa, baking soda and cinnamon, if desired. Add to butter mixture, blending well. Stir in peanut butter chips. Fill muffin cups ¾ full with batter.

3. Bake 22 to 26 minutes or until wooden pick inserted in center comes out almost clean. Cool slightly in pan on wire rack. Sprinkle muffin tops with powdered sugar, if desired. Serve warm. *Makes 12 to 15 muffins*

Fudgey Chocolate Chip Muffins: Omit Peanut Butter Chips. Add 1 cup HERSHEY'S Semi-Sweet Chocolate Chips.

Fudgey Peanut Butter Chip Muffins

Chocolate Malts

Cupcakes
  1¾ **cups cake flour**
   ¾ **teaspoon baking soda**
   ½ **teaspoon salt**
  1¼ **cups granulated sugar, divided**
   2 **eggs, at room temperature**
   ⅓ **cup vegetable oil**
   1 **cup low-fat buttermilk**
   ¼ **cup chocolate malted milk powder**
   1 **teaspoon vanilla**

Marshmallow Frosting
   1 **cup thawed frozen whipped topping**
   ½ **cup marshmallow creme**
    Chopped malted milk balls
    Additional chocolate malted milk powder

1. Preheat oven to 350°F. Grease and flour 12 standard (2½-inch) muffin pan cups or line with paper baking cups; set aside.

2. For cupcakes, sift flour, baking soda and salt together in bowl. Stir in ¾ cup sugar; set aside. Beat eggs and remaining ½ cup sugar in large bowl with electric mixer at medium-high speed 3 minutes or until light and glossy. Reduce speed to low; beat in ⅓ of flour mixture until thick. Add oil; beat until smooth. Combine buttermilk, malted milk powder and vanilla in small bowl; stir until well blended. Add ⅓ of buttermilk mixture to egg mixture; beat until smooth. Add remaining flour mixture alternating with remaining buttermilk mixture, beating well after each addition.

3. Divide batter evenly among prepared muffin cups. Bake about 25 minutes or until toothpicks inserted into centers come out clean. Cool in pan on wire rack 15 minutes. Remove from pan to wire rack; cool completely.

4. For marshmallow frosting, combine whipped topping and marshmallow creme in medium bowl; stir until well blended and smooth. Spread frosting over cupcakes. Sprinkle with malted milk balls and dust with additional malted milk powder.

Makes 12 cupcakes

Chocolate Malts

Gingerbread Streusel Raisin Muffins

     1 cup raisins
  ½ cup boiling water
  ⅓ cup margarine or butter, softened
  ¾ cup GRANDMA'S® Molasses (Unsulphured)
     1 egg
     2 cups all-purpose flour
  1½ teaspoons baking soda
     1 teaspoon cinnamon
     1 teaspoon ginger
  ½ teaspoon salt

Topping
  ⅓ cup all-purpose flour
  ¼ cup firmly packed brown sugar
  ¼ cup chopped nuts
     3 tablespoons margarine or butter
     1 teaspoon cinnamon

Preheat oven to 375°F. Grease bottoms only of 12 muffin cups or line with paper baking cups. In small bowl, cover raisins with boiling water; let stand 5 minutes. In large bowl, beat ⅓ cup margarine and molasses until fluffy. Add egg; beat well. Stir in 2 cups flour, baking soda, 1 teaspoon cinnamon, ginger and salt. Blend just until dry ingredients are moistened. Gently stir in raisins and water. Fill prepared muffin cups ¾ full. For topping, combine all ingredients in small bowl. Sprinkle over muffins.

Bake 20 to 25 minutes or until toothpick inserted in centers comes out clean. Cool 5 minutes; remove from pan. Serve warm.   *Makes 12 muffins*

Gingerbread Streusel Raisin Muffins

Pesto Surprise Muffins

2 cups all-purpose flour
3 tablespoons grated Parmesan cheese, divided
1 tablespoon baking powder
½ teaspoon salt
1 cup milk
¼ cup vegetable oil
1 egg
¼ cup prepared pesto sauce

Preheat oven to 400°F. Grease 12 standard (2½-inch) muffin pan cups or line with paper baking cups. Combine flour, 2 tablespoons cheese, baking powder and salt in large bowl. Combine milk, oil and egg in small bowl; stir until blended. Add to flour mixture; stir just until moistened. *Do not overmix.* Spoon into prepared muffin cups, filling ⅓ full. Stir pesto sauce; spoon 1 teaspoon sauce into each muffin cup. Spoon remaining batter evenly over pesto sauce. Sprinkle remaining 1 tablespoon cheese evenly over muffins. Bake 25 to 30 minutes or until toothpicks inserted into centers come out clean. Cool in pan on wire rack 5 minutes. Remove from pan; cool completely on wire rack. *Makes 12 muffins*

Quick & Easy Pumpkin Cupcakes

1 package (18.25 ounces) spice cake mix
1 can (15 ounces) LIBBY'S® 100% Pure Pumpkin
3 eggs
⅓ cup vegetable oil
⅓ cup water
1 container (16 ounces) prepared cream cheese or vanilla frosting
Assorted sprinkles

PREHEAT oven to 350°F. Paper-line or grease 24 muffin cups.

BLEND cake mix, pumpkin, eggs, vegetable oil and water in large mixer bowl until moistened. Beat on medium speed for 2 minutes. Pour batter into prepared muffin cups, filling ¾ full.

BAKE for 18 to 23 minutes or until wooden pick inserted in center comes out clean. Cool in pan on wire rack for 10 minutes; remove to wire racks to cool completely. Spread cupcakes with frosting. Decorate as desired. *Makes 14 cupcakes*

Pesto Surprise Muffins

Mocha-Macadamia Nut Muffins

1¼ **cups all-purpose flour**
⅔ **cup sugar**
2½ **tablespoons unsweetened cocoa powder**
1 **teaspoon baking soda**
¼ **teaspoon salt**
⅔ **cup buttermilk***
3 **tablespoons butter, melted**
1 **egg, beaten**
1 **tablespoon instant coffee granules dissolved in 1 tablespoon hot water**
¾ **teaspoon vanilla**
½ **cup coarsely chopped macadamia nuts**
Powdered sugar (optional)

Soured fresh milk can be substituted for buttermilk. To sour milk, combine 2 teaspoons lemon juice plus enough milk to equal ⅔ cup. Stir; let stand 5 minutes before using.

1. Preheat oven to 400°F. Lightly grease 12 standard (2½-inch) muffin pan cups or line with paper baking cups.

2. Combine flour, sugar, cocoa, baking soda and salt in large bowl. Whisk together buttermilk, butter, egg, coffee mixture and vanilla in small bowl until blended. Stir into flour mixture just until moistened. Fold in macadamia nuts. Spoon evenly into prepared muffin cups.

3. Bake 13 to 17 minutes or until toothpicks inserted into centers come out clean. Cool in pan on wire rack 5 minutes. Remove from pan to wire rack; cool 10 minutes. Sprinkle with powdered sugar, if desired. *Makes 12 muffins*

Mocha-Macadamia Nut Muffins

Blueberry Crisp Cupcakes

Cupcakes
  2 cups all-purpose flour
  2 teaspoons baking powder
  ¼ teaspoon salt
  1¾ cups granulated sugar
  ½ cup (1 stick) butter, softened
  ¾ cup milk
  1½ teaspoons vanilla
  3 egg whites
  3 cups fresh or frozen (unthawed) blueberries

Streusel
  ⅓ cup all-purpose flour
  ¼ cup uncooked old-fashioned or quick oats
  ¼ cup packed light brown sugar
  ½ teaspoon ground cinnamon
  ¼ cup (½ stick) butter, softened
  ½ cup chopped walnuts or pecans

1. Preheat oven to 350°F. Lightly grease 30 standard (2½-inch) muffin pan cups or line with paper baking cups.

2. For cupcakes, combine 2 cups flour, baking powder and salt in medium bowl; mix well. Set aside. Beat granulated sugar and ½ cup butter in large bowl with electric mixer at medium speed 1 minute. Add milk and vanilla. Beat at low speed 30 seconds. Gradually beat in flour mixture; beat at medium speed 2 minutes. Add egg whites; beat 1 minute. Spoon batter into prepared muffin cups filling ½ full. Spoon blueberries over batter. Bake 10 minutes.

3. Meanwhile for streusel, combine ⅓ cup flour, oats, brown sugar and cinnamon in small bowl; mix well. Cut in ¼ cup butter with pastry blender or two knives until mixture resembles coarse crumbs. Stir in chopped nuts.

4. Sprinkle streusel over partially baked cupcakes. Return to oven; bake 18 to 20 minutes or until golden brown and toothpicks inserted into centers come out clean. Cool in pans on wire racks 10 minutes. Remove from pans to wire racks; cool completely.

Makes 30 cupcakes

Blueberry Crisp Cupcakes

Vanilla-Strawberry Cupcakes

Cupcakes
>   **2 cups all-purpose flour**
>   **2 teaspoons baking powder**
>   **¼ teaspoon salt**
>   **1¾ cups granulated sugar**
>   **½ cup (1 stick) butter, softened**
>   **¾ cup milk**
>   **1½ teaspoons vanilla**
>   **3 egg whites**
>   **½ cup strawberry preserves**

Frosting
>   **1 package (8 ounces) cream cheese, chilled and cut into cubes**
>   **¼ cup (½ stick) butter, softened**
>   **2 teaspoons vanilla**
>   **2 cups powdered sugar**
>   **1 to 1½ cups sliced fresh strawberries**

1. Preheat oven to 350°F. Lightly grease 28 standard (2½-inch) muffin pan cups or line with paper baking cups.

2. For cupcakes, combine flour, baking powder and salt in medium bowl; mix well and set aside. Beat granulated sugar and ½ cup butter in large bowl with electric mixer at medium speed 1 minute. Add milk and 1½ teaspoons vanilla. Beat at low speed 30 seconds. Gradually beat in flour mixture; beat at medium speed 2 minutes. Add egg whites; beat 1 minute.

3. Spoon batter into prepared muffin cups filling ½ full. Drop 1 teaspoon preserves on top of batter; swirl into batter with toothpick. Bake 20 to 22 minutes or until toothpicks inserted into centers come out clean. Cool in pans on wire racks 10 minutes. Remove from pans to wire racks; cool completely.

4. For frosting, process cream cheese, ¼ cup butter and 2 teaspoons vanilla in food processor just until blended. Add powdered sugar; pulse just until sugar is incorporated. (Do not overmix or frosting will be too soft to spread).

5. Spread frosting over cooled cupcakes; decorate with sliced strawberries. Serve immediately or refrigerate up to 8 hours before serving.   *Makes 28 cupcakes*

Vanilla-Strawberry Cupcakes

Brunchtime Sour Cream Cupcakes

1 cup (2 sticks) butter, softened
2 cups plus 4 teaspoons sugar, divided
2 eggs
1 cup sour cream
1 teaspoon almond extract
2 cups all-purpose flour
1 teaspoon salt
½ teaspoon baking soda
1 cup chopped walnuts
1½ teaspoons ground cinnamon
⅛ teaspoon ground nutmeg

1. Preheat oven to 350°F. Lightly grease 18 standard (2½-inch) muffin pan cups or line with paper baking cups.

2. Beat butter and 2 cups sugar in large bowl. Add eggs, one at a time, beating well after each addition. Blend in sour cream and almond extract. Combine flour, salt and baking soda in medium bowl. Add to butter mixture; mix well.

3. Stir together remaining 4 teaspoons sugar, walnuts, cinnamon and nutmeg in small bowl.

4. Fill prepared muffin cups ⅓ full with batter; sprinkle evenly with ⅔ of the walnut mixture. Cover with remaining batter. Sprinkle with remaining walnut mixture.

5. Bake 25 to 30 minutes or until toothpicks inserted into centers come out clean. Remove cupcakes from pan; cool on wire rack.   *Makes 1½ dozen cupcakes*

Brunchtime Sour Cream Cupcakes

luscious cakes & desserts

Chocolate Lovers' Cake

> **1 package (18.25 ounces) chocolate cake mix, plus ingredients to prepare mix**
> **3 tablespoons seedless raspberry preserves, melted**
> **Chocolate Ganache (recipe follows)**
> **⅔ cup sweetened condensed milk**
> **1 cup (6 ounces) semisweet chocolate chips**
> **1 tablespoon butter**
> **Chocolate Shapes (page 41)**

1. Prepare cake mix according to package directions for two 8- or 9-inch layers. After removing layers from pans, poke holes all over top of each layer with toothpick or skewer. Brush melted preserves over warm cake layers. Set aside to cool completely.

2. Prepare Chocolate Ganache. While ganache cools, combine sweetened condensed milk, chocolate chips and butter in small heavy saucepan. Cook over low heat until chips are melted and mixture is smooth. Cool slightly.

3. Place one cake layer on serving plate; spread sweetened condensed milk mixture evenly over cake. Top with second cake layer. Frost cake with Chocolate Ganache; top with Chocolate Shapes. *Makes 12 servings*

Chocolate Ganache: Combine ¾ cup heavy cream, 1 tablespoon butter and 1 tablespoon granulated sugar in small saucepan; bring to a boil over high heat, stirring until sugar is dissolved. Place 1½ cups semisweet chocolate chips in medium bowl. Pour cream mixture over chocolate and let stand 5 minutes. Stir until smooth; let stand 15 minutes or until ganache reaches desired consistency. (Ganache will thicken as it cools.) Makes about 1½ cups.

Chocolate Lovers' Cake

Zesty Lemon Pound Cake

> 1 cup (6 ounces) **NESTLÉ® TOLL HOUSE®** Premier White Morsels or
>   3 bars (6-ounce box) **NESTLÉ® TOLL HOUSE®** Premier White
>   Baking Bars, broken into pieces
> 2½ cups all-purpose flour
>   1 teaspoon baking powder
>   ½ teaspoon salt
>   1 cup (2 sticks) butter, softened
> 1½ cups granulated sugar
>   2 teaspoons vanilla extract
>   3 eggs
>   3 to 4 tablespoons grated lemon peel (about 3 medium lemons)
> 1⅓ cups buttermilk
>   1 cup powdered sugar
>   3 tablespoons fresh lemon juice

PREHEAT oven to 350°F. Grease and flour 12-cup Bundt pan.

MELT morsels in medium, uncovered, microwave-safe bowl on MEDIUM–HIGH (70%) power for 1 minute. STIR. Morsels may retain some of their original shape. If necessary, microwave at additional 10- to 15-second intervals, stirring just until morsels are melted. Cool slightly.

COMBINE flour, baking powder and salt in small bowl. Beat butter, granulated sugar and vanilla extract in large mixer bowl until creamy. Beat in eggs, one at a time, beating well after each addition. Beat in lemon peel and melted morsels. Gradually beat in flour mixture alternately with buttermilk. Pour into prepared Bundt pan.

BAKE for 50 to 55 minutes or until wooden pick inserted in cake comes out clean. Cool in pan on wire rack for 10 minutes. Combine powdered sugar and lemon juice in small bowl. Make holes in cake with wooden pick; pour *half* of lemon glaze over cake. Let stand for 5 minutes. Invert onto plate. Make holes in top of cake; pour *remaining* glaze over cake. Cool completely before serving.   *Makes 16 servings*

Zesty Lemon Pound Cake

Passionate Profiteroles

Vanilla Custard Filling (recipe follows)
⅔ cup water
7 tablespoons plus 2 teaspoons I CAN'T BELIEVE IT'S NOT BUTTER!®
Spread, divided
1 tablespoon sugar
¼ teaspoon salt
¾ cup all-purpose flour
4 eggs
1 square (1 ounce) semi-sweet chocolate

Prepare Vanilla Custard Filling. Preheat oven to 400°F. Lightly grease baking sheet; set aside. In 2½-quart saucepan, bring water, 7 tablespoons I Can't Believe It's Not Butter!® Spread, sugar and salt to a boil over high heat. Remove from heat and immediately stir in flour. With wooden spoon, cook flour mixture over medium heat, stirring constantly, 5 minutes or until film forms on bottom of pan. Remove from heat; stir in eggs, one at a time, beating well after each addition. Immediately drop by heaping tablespoonfuls onto prepared baking sheet. Place baking sheet on middle rack in oven.

Bake 20 minutes. Decrease oven temperature to 350°F and bake an additional 20 minutes. Turn off oven without opening door and let profiteroles stand in oven 10 minutes. Cool completely on wire rack. To fill, slice off top ⅓ of profiteroles and set aside. Fill with Vanilla Custard Filling. Replace profiterole tops.

In small microwave-safe bowl, microwave chocolate and remaining 2 teaspoons I Can't Believe It's Not Butter! Spread at HIGH (Full Power) 30 seconds or until chocolate is melted; stir until smooth. Drizzle chocolate mixture over profiteroles, then sprinkle, if desired, with toasted sliced almonds. *Makes 16 servings*

Vanilla Custard Filling

1 package (3.4 ounces) instant vanilla pudding
1 cup milk
3 to 4 tablespoons hazelnut, coffee, almond, orange or cherry
liqueur (optional)
½ teaspoon vanilla extract
2 cups whipped cream or non-dairy whipped topping

In medium bowl, with wire whisk, blend pudding mix, milk, liqueur and vanilla. Fold in whipped cream. Cover with plastic wrap and refrigerate 1 hour or until set.

Passionate Profiteroles

Gingerbread Cake with Lemon Sauce

Cake
    ¼ **Butter Flavor CRISCO® Stick or** ¼ **cup Butter Flavor CRISCO®**
        all-vegetable shortening
    ¼ **cup firmly packed light brown sugar**
    ¼ **cup granulated sugar**
    1 **egg, lightly beaten**
    ½ **cup buttermilk**
    ¼ **cup light molasses**
    1 **cup all-purpose flour**
    2 **teaspoons ground ginger**
    1 **teaspoon ground cinnamon**
    ½ **teaspoon baking soda**
    ¼ **teaspoon ground cloves**
    ¼ **teaspoon freshly grated nutmeg**
    ¼ **teaspoon salt**

Lemon Sauce
    ½ **cup granulated sugar**
    ¼ **cup unsalted butter**
    3 **tablespoons fresh lemon juice**
    1 **teaspoon vanilla**

1. Heat oven to 375°F. Lightly spray 8-inch square or round cake pan with CRISCO® No-Stick Cooking Spray; set aside.

2. For cake, combine ¼ cup shortening, brown sugar and ¼ cup granulated sugar in large bowl. Beat at medium speed with electric mixer until well blended. Beat in egg, buttermilk and molasses until well blended.

3. Combine flour, ginger, cinnamon, baking soda, cloves, nutmeg and salt in medium bowl. Add to creamed mixture; mix well. Pour batter into prepared pan.

4. Bake at 375°F for 20 to 25 minutes or until toothpick inserted in center comes out clean. Cool in pan 15 minutes. Turn out onto cooling rack.

5. For lemon sauce, combine all ingredients in small saucepan. Bring to a boil over medium-high heat, stirring constantly. Reduce heat to low; simmer 5 minutes or until sauce is slightly thickened. Serve sauce over each slice of cake. Garnish with freshly grated lemon peel, if desired. *Makes 6 to 8 servings*

Gingerbread Cake with Lemon Sauce

Triple Chip Cheesecake

Crust
1¾ cups chocolate graham cracker crumbs
⅓ cup butter or margarine, melted

Filling
3 packages (8 ounces *each*) cream cheese, softened
¾ cup granulated sugar
½ cup sour cream
3 tablespoons all-purpose flour
1½ teaspoons vanilla extract
3 eggs
1 cup (6 ounces) NESTLÉ® TOLL HOUSE® Butterscotch Flavored Morsels
1 cup (6 ounces) NESTLÉ® TOLL HOUSE® Semi-Sweet Chocolate Morsels
1 cup (6 ounces) NESTLÉ® TOLL HOUSE® Premier White Morsels

Topping
1 tablespoon *each* NESTLÉ® TOLL HOUSE® Butterscotch Flavored Morsels, Semi-Sweet Chocolate Morsels and Premier White Morsels

PREHEAT oven to 300°F. Grease 9-inch springform pan.

For Crust

COMBINE crumbs and butter in small bowl. Press onto bottom and 1 inch up side of prepared pan.

For Filling

BEAT cream cheese and granulated sugar in large mixer bowl until smooth. Add sour cream, flour and vanilla extract; mix well. Add eggs; beat on low speed until combined.

MELT butterscotch morsels according to package directions. Stir until smooth. Add 1½ *cups* batter to melted morsels. Pour into crust. Repeat procedure with semi-sweet morsels. Carefully spoon over butterscotch layer. Melt Premier White morsels according to package directions and blend into *remaining* batter in mixer bowl. Carefully pour over semi-sweet layer.

BAKE for 1 hour and 10 to 15 minutes or until center is almost set. Cool in pan on wire rack for 10 minutes. Run knife around edge of cheesecake. Let stand for 1 hour.

continued on page 182

Triple Chip Cheesecake

Triple Chip Cheesecake, continued

For Topping
PLACE each flavor of morsels separately into three small, *heavy-duty* resealable plastic food storage bags. Microwave on HIGH (100%) power for 20 seconds; knead bags to mix. Microwave at additional 10-second intervals, kneading until smooth. Cut small hole in corner of each bag; squeeze to drizzle over cheesecake. Refrigerate for at least 3 hours or overnight. Remove side of pan.   *Makes 12 to 16 servings*

Raisin Pear Crisp

   8 **medium pears, quartered, cored and sliced ¼ inch thick**
   1 **cup SUN-MAID® Raisins**
   ½ **cup granulated sugar**
   2 **tablespoons all-purpose flour**
   2 **tablespoons lemon juice**
   ¾ **cup packed brown sugar**
   ¾ **cup old-fashioned oats**
   ⅔ **cup all-purpose flour**
   1 **teaspoon cinnamon**
   6 **tablespoons butter, at room temperature**
   ¼ **cup chopped hazelnuts**

HEAT oven to 350°F. Butter a 13×9-inch baking dish.

GENTLY mix pears, raisins, sugar, 2 tablespoons flour and lemon juice. Place in prepared dish.

COMBINE brown sugar, oats, ⅔ cup flour and cinnamon in a medium bowl. With pastry blender or fingers, mix in butter until crumbly.

MIX in hazelnuts.

CRUMBLE mixture over fruit.

BAKE about 40 minutes until golden brown and fruit is bubbly. Serve warm.
                                                              Makes 8 servings

Prep Time: 20 minutes
Baking Time: 40 minutes

Bread Pudding with Brandy Apricot Sauce

5 cups cubed dry French bread with crusts
3 eggs
2 cups 2% milk
¾ cup packed brown sugar
½ cup granulated sugar
3 tablespoons butter, melted
1 tablespoon vanilla
1 teaspoon ground cinnamon
⅓ cup raisins
Brandy Apricot Sauce (recipe follows)

Spread bread cubes in 8×8-inch baking pan coated with nonstick cooking spray.

In medium bowl, beat eggs until frothy; add milk, sugars, butter, vanilla and cinnamon. Beat until well mixed. Stir in raisins. Pour over bread, pressing bread lightly until coated. Let stand 40 minutes, occasionally pressing bread lightly to soak. Bake at 325°F for 50 minutes. *Increase oven temperature to 400°F.* Bake bread pudding 10 minutes or until browned and puffy. Serve warm or at room temperature with Brandy Apricot Sauce.

Makes 12 servings

Brandy Apricot Sauce

1 cup (12-ounce jar) apricot preserves
¼ cup water
3 tablespoons brandy or orange juice

Bring apricot preserves and water to a boil in small saucepan. Cook 1 minute. Stir in brandy. Serve warm over bread pudding.

Favorite recipe from **North Dakota Wheat Commission**

Blueberry Streusel Cobbler

1 pint fresh or frozen blueberries
1 (14-ounce) can EAGLE BRAND® Sweetened Condensed Milk
(NOT evaporated milk)
2 teaspoons grated lemon peel
¾ cup (1½ sticks) plus 2 tablespoons cold butter or margarine,
divided
2 cups biscuit baking mix, divided
½ cup firmly packed light brown sugar
½ cup chopped nuts
Vanilla ice cream
Blueberry Sauce (recipe follows)

1. Preheat oven to 325°F. In medium mixing bowl, combine blueberries, Eagle Brand and lemon peel.

2. In large mixing bowl, cut ¾ cup butter into 1½ cups biscuit mix until crumbly; add blueberry mixture. Spread in greased 9-inch square baking pan.

3. In small mixing bowl, combine remaining ½ cup biscuit mix and brown sugar; cut in remaining 2 tablespoons butter until crumbly. Add nuts. Sprinkle over cobbler.

4. Bake 1 hour and 10 minutes or until golden. Serve warm with vanilla ice cream and Blueberry Sauce. Refrigerate leftovers.   *Makes 8 to 12 servings*

Blueberry Sauce: In large saucepan over medium heat, combine ½ cup sugar, 1 tablespoon cornstarch, ½ teaspoon ground cinnamon and ¼ teaspoon ground nutmeg. Gradually add ½ cup water. Cook and stir until thickened. Stir in 1 pint blueberries; cook and stir until hot. Makes about 1⅔ cups.

Prep Time: 15 minutes
Bake Time: 1 hour and 10 minutes

Blueberry Streusel Cobbler

Peanut Butter Delight Cake

Cake
　　1 cup granulated sugar
　　¾ cup Butter Flavor CRISCO® Stick or ¾ cup Butter Flavor CRISCO®
　　　　all-vegetable shortening plus additional for greasing
　　¾ cup JIF® Creamy Peanut Butter
　　½ cup firmly packed light brown sugar
　　1½ teaspoons vanilla
　　3 eggs
　　2¾ cups all-purpose flour
　　2 teaspoons baking powder
　　1 teaspoon baking soda
　　½ teaspoon salt
　　1 cup buttermilk or sour milk*
　　¾ cup chocolate syrup

Glaze
　　1 cup confectioners' sugar
　　¼ cup chocolate syrup
　　1 teaspoon vanilla
　　2 to 4 tablespoons chopped dry-roasted peanuts

*To sour milk: combine 1 tablespoon white vinegar plus enough milk to equal 1 cup. Stir. Let stand 5 minutes before using.

1. Heat oven to 350°F. Grease 10-inch (12-cup) bundt pan with shortening and flour lightly. For cake, combine granulated sugar, ¾ cup shortening, JIF® peanut butter and brown sugar in large bowl. Beat at low speed of electric mixer until creamy. Add vanilla and eggs, 1 at a time, beating well after each addition. Combine flour, baking powder, baking soda and salt in medium bowl. Add to peanut butter mixture alternately with buttermilk, beating after each addition until well blended. Spoon 2 cups batter into medium bowl. Stir in ¾ cup chocolate syrup. Spoon plain batter into pan. Spoon chocolate batter over plain batter. Do not mix.

2. Bake at 350°F for 1 hour and 10 to 20 minutes or until toothpick inserted in center comes out clean. (Cake will rise, then fall during baking.) Do not overbake. Cool 45 minutes on wire rack before removing from pan. Place cake, fluted side up, on serving plate. Cool completely.

3. For glaze, combine confectioners' sugar, ¼ cup chocolate syrup and vanilla in small bowl. Stir to blend. Add water, 1 drop at a time, until glaze is of desired consistency. Spoon over top of cake. Sprinkle with nuts. *Makes 12 to 16 servings*

Peanut Butter Delight Cake

Fruit-Filled Chocolate Chip Meringue Nests

Meringues
- 4 egg whites
- ½ teaspoon salt
- ½ teaspoon cream of tartar
- 1 cup granulated sugar
- 2 cups (12-ounce package) NESTLÉ® TOLL HOUSE® Semi-Sweet Chocolate Morsels

Chocolate Sauce
- ⅔ cup (5 fluid-ounce can) NESTLÉ® CARNATION® Evaporated Milk
- 1 cup (6 ounces) NESTLÉ® TOLL HOUSE® Semi-Sweet Chocolate Morsels
- 1 tablespoon granulated sugar
- 1 teaspoon vanilla extract
- Pinch salt
- 3 cups fresh fruit or berries (whole blackberries, blueberries or raspberries, sliced kiwi, peaches or strawberries)

For Meringues

PREHEAT oven to 300°F. Lightly grease baking sheets.

BEAT egg whites, salt and cream of tartar in large mixer bowl until soft peaks form. Gradually add sugar; beat until sugar is dissolved. Gently fold in morsels. Spread meringue into ten 3-inch nests with deep wells about 2 inches apart on prepared baking sheets.

BAKE for 35 to 45 minutes or until meringues are dry and crisp. Cool on baking sheets for 5 minutes; remove to wire racks to cool completely.

For Chocolate Sauce

HEAT evaporated milk to a boil in small, *heavy-duty* saucepan. Stir in morsels. Cook, stirring constantly, until mixture is slightly thickened and smooth. Remove from heat; stir in sugar, vanilla extract and salt.

FILL meringues with fruit and drizzle with Chocolate Sauce; serve immediately.

Makes 10 servings

Fruit-Filled Chocolate Chip Meringue Nests

Coconut Pound Cake

Cake
 2 cups granulated sugar
 1 Butter Flavor CRISCO® Stick or 1 cup Butter Flavor CRISCO®
  all-vegetable shortening plus additional for greasing
 5 eggs
 1½ teaspoons coconut extract
 2¼ cups all-purpose flour
 1½ teaspoons baking powder
 ½ teaspoon salt
 1 cup buttermilk or sour milk*
 1 cup shredded coconut, chopped

Glaze
 ½ cup sugar
 ¼ cup water
 1½ teaspoons coconut extract

Garnish (optional)
 Whipped topping or whipped cream and assorted fresh fruit

To sour milk: combine 1 tablespoon white vinegar plus enough milk to equal 1 cup. Stir. Let stand 5 minutes before using.

1. Heat oven to 350°F. Grease 10-inch tube pan with shortening; flour lightly. Place cooling rack on countertop to cool cake.

2. For cake, combine 2 cups sugar and 1 cup shortening in large bowl. Beat at medium speed with electric mixer until blended. Add eggs, 1 at a time, beating slightly after each addition. Beat in 1½ teaspoons coconut extract. Combine flour, baking powder and salt in medium bowl. Add alternately with buttermilk to creamed mixture, beating at low speed after each addition until well blended. Add coconut. Mix until blended. Spoon into prepared pan.

3. Bake at 350°F for 50 minutes or until toothpick inserted in center comes out clean. *Do not overbake.* Remove to wire rack. Cool 5 minutes. Remove cake from pan. Place on serving plate. Use toothpick to poke 12 to 15 holes in top of cake.

4. For glaze, combine ½ cup sugar, water and 1½ teaspoons coconut extract in small saucepan. Cook and stir over medium heat until mixture comes to a boil. Remove from heat. Cool 15 minutes. Spoon over cake. Cool completely.

5. For optional garnish, place spoonfuls of whipped topping and assorted fresh fruit on each serving.   *Makes one 10-inch tube cake (12 to 16 servings)*

Coconut Pound Cake

Walnut-Orange Torte with Apricot Cream

Torte
- **6 eggs, separated**
- **½ cup packed dark brown sugar**
- **1 tablespoon grated orange peel**
- **2 tablespoons orange juice**
- **1 teaspoon vanilla**
- **1 cup ground walnuts**
- **½ cup plain dry bread crumbs**
- **⅛ teaspoon salt**
- **3 tablespoons granulated sugar**

Apricot Cream
- **1½ cups whipping cream**
- **2 tablespoons powdered sugar**
- **1 cup apricot spreadable fruit**

Sugared Walnuts
- **1 egg white**
- **1½ cups (6 ounces) walnut halves**
- **½ cup granulated sugar**

1. For torte, preheat oven to 350°F. Grease two 8×1¾-inch round cake pans. Line bottoms with parchment paper. Mix egg yolks, brown sugar and orange peel in bowl; beat until thick and pale. Beat in juice and vanilla. Mix ground walnuts and bread crumbs; fold into yolk mixture. In clean bowl, beat 6 egg whites and salt until soft peaks form. Add granulated sugar; beat until glossy and stiff but not dry. Fold ⅓ of egg whites into yolk mixture; fold in remaining whites. Divide batter between prepared pans.

2. Bake 20 to 22 minutes until golden and centers spring back when lightly touched. Cool in pans 10 to 15 minutes. Remove from pans; cool completely on wire racks.

3. For apricot cream, beat cream and powdered sugar in large bowl until stiff peaks form. Place spreadable fruit in bowl. Stir ⅓ whipped cream into fruit; fold into remaining whipped cream. Split cake layers in half horizontally with serrated knife. Fill and frost cake layers with apricot cream.

4. For sugared walnuts, beat egg white in bowl; stir in walnut halves. Add sugar; stir to coat. Transfer to foil-lined baking sheet with slotted spatula, letting excess sugar mixture drip off. Bake in 300°F oven 30 minutes until dry and crisp; cool completely.

5. Place sugared walnuts around top edge of cake. Crush remaining nuts; press around bottom of cake. Refrigerate until ready to serve. *Makes 8 servings*

Walnut-Orange Torte with Apricot Cream

Chocolate Intensity

Cake
> 4 bars (8-ounce box) NESTLÉ® TOLL HOUSE® Unsweetened Chocolate Baking Bars, broken into pieces
> ½ cup (1 stick) butter, softened
> 1½ cups granulated sugar
> 3 eggs
> 2 teaspoons vanilla extract
> ⅔ cup all-purpose flour
> Powdered sugar (optional)

Coffee Crème Anglaise Sauce
> 4 egg yolks, lightly beaten
> ⅓ cup granulated sugar
> 1 tablespoon TASTER'S CHOICE® 100% Pure Instant Coffee
> 1½ cups milk
> 1 teaspoon vanilla extract

PREHEAT oven to 350°F. Grease 9-inch springform pan.

For Cake

MICROWAVE baking bars in medium, uncovered, microwave-safe bowl on HIGH (100%) power for 1 minute. STIR. The bars may retain some of their original shape. If necessary, microwave at additional 10- to 15-second intervals, stirring just until smooth. Cool to lukewarm.

BEAT butter, granulated sugar, eggs and vanilla extract in small mixer bowl for about 4 minutes or until thick and pale yellow. Beat in melted chocolate. Gradually beat in flour. Spread into prepared springform pan.

BAKE for 25 to 28 minutes or until wooden pick inserted in center comes out moist. Cool in pan on wire rack for 15 minutes. Loosen and remove side of pan; cool completely. Sprinkle with powdered sugar; serve with Coffee Crème Anglaise Sauce.

For Coffee Crème Anglaise Sauce

PLACE egg yolks in medium bowl. Combine granulated sugar and Taster's Choice in medium saucepan; stir in milk. Cook over medium heat, stirring constantly, until mixture comes just to a very gentle boil. Remove from heat. Gradually whisk *half* of hot milk mixture into egg yolks; return mixture to saucepan. Cook, stirring constantly, for 3 to 4 minutes or until mixture is slightly thickened. Strain into small bowl; stir in vanilla extract. Cover; refrigerate. *Makes 10 to 12 servings*

Chocolate Intensity

Spiced Cranberry-Apple Sour Cream Cobbler

4 cups cranberries, washed
6 Granny Smith apples, peeled and thinly sliced
2 cups firmly packed light brown sugar
1 teaspoon ground cinnamon
1 teaspoon vanilla
¼ teaspoon ground cloves
2 cups plus 1 tablespoon all-purpose flour, divided
4 tablespoons butter, cut into pieces
2 teaspoons double acting baking powder
1 teaspoon salt
½ CRISCO® Stick or ½ cup CRISCO® all-vegetable shortening
1½ cups sour cream
2 teaspoons granulated sugar
Cinnamon or vanilla ice cream

1. Heat oven to 400°F. Combine cranberries, apples, brown sugar, cinnamon, vanilla, ground cloves and 1 tablespoon flour in 3-quart baking dish; mix evenly. Dot top with butter.

2. Stir together remaining 2 cups flour, baking powder and salt in medium bowl. Cut in ½ cup shortening using pastry blender or 2 knives until medium-size crumbs form. Add sour cream; blend well. (Dough will be sticky.) Drop dough by spoonfuls on top of fruit mixture. Sprinkle with granulated sugar. Bake at 400°F for 20 to 30 minutes, on middle rack, until top is golden. Serve with cinnamon or vanilla ice cream, if desired. *Makes 6 to 8 servings*

tip

Lucky enough to have some leftover cobbler? Store it in the refrigerator for up to two days. Reheat it, covered, in a 350°F oven until warm.

Spiced Cranberry-Apple Sour Cream Cobbler

Carrot Cake

       4 eggs
1¼ cups vegetable oil
   2 cups all-purpose flour
1½ cups sugar
   2 teaspoons baking powder
   2 teaspoons ground cinnamon
   1 teaspoon baking soda
¼ teaspoon salt
2½ cups shredded carrots (about 7 medium)
   1 cup coarsely chopped pecans or walnuts
      Cream Cheese Icing (recipe follows)

1. Preheat oven to 350°F. Grease and flour 13×9-inch baking pan.

2. Beat eggs and oil in small bowl. Combine flour, sugar, baking powder, cinnamon, baking soda and salt in large bowl. Add egg mixture; mix well. Stir in carrots and pecans. Pour into prepared pan.

3. Bake 40 to 45 minutes or until toothpick inserted into center comes out clean. Cool cake completely in pan on wire rack.

4. Prepare Cream Cheese Icing. Spread over cooled cake. Garnish as desired.

Makes 8 servings

Cream Cheese Icing

   1 package (8 ounces) cream cheese, softened
½ cup (1 stick) butter, softened
   1 teaspoon vanilla
   4 cups powdered sugar

Beat cream cheese, butter and vanilla in large bowl with electric mixer at medium speed until smooth, scraping down side of bowl occasionally. Gradually add powdered sugar. Beat at low speed until well blended, scraping down side of bowl occasionally.

Makes about 1½ cups icing

Carrot Cake

Caramel Flan

1 cup sugar, divided
2 cups half-and-half
1 cup milk
1½ teaspoons vanilla
6 eggs
2 egg yolks
Hot water
Fresh whole and sliced strawberries for garnish

1. Preheat oven to 325°F. Heat 5½- to 6-cup ring mold in oven 10 minutes or until hot.

2. Heat ½ cup sugar in heavy, medium skillet over medium-high heat 5 to 8 minutes or until sugar is completely melted and deep amber color, stirring frequently. *Do not allow sugar to burn.*

3. Immediately pour caramelized sugar into ring mold. Holding mold with potholder, quickly rotate to coat bottom and sides evenly with sugar. Place mold on wire rack. *Caution: Caramelized sugar is very hot; do not touch it.*

4. Combine half-and-half and milk in heavy 2-quart saucepan. Heat over medium heat until almost simmering; remove from heat. Add remaining ½ cup sugar and vanilla; stir until sugar is dissolved.

5. Lightly beat eggs and egg yolks in large bowl until blended but not foamy; gradually stir in milk mixture. Pour custard into ring mold.

6. Place mold in large baking pan; pour hot water into baking pan to depth of ½ inch. Bake 35 to 40 minutes or until knife inserted into center of custard comes out clean.

7. Remove mold from water bath; place on wire rack. Let stand 30 minutes. Cover and refrigerate 1½ to 2 hours or until thoroughly chilled.

8. To serve, loosen inner and outer edges of flan with tip of small knife. Cover mold with rimmed serving plate; invert and lift off mold. Garnish with strawberries, if desired. Spoon melted caramel over each serving. *Makes 6 to 8 servings*

Caramel Flan

Berry Shortcakes

1¾ cups all-purpose flour
1 tablespoon baking powder
⅛ teaspoon salt
½ cup (1 stick) cold butter
½ cup milk
1 teaspoon vanilla
1 egg
1 teaspoon water
1 cup sliced strawberries
1 cup raspberries
1 cup blueberries
3 tablespoons no-sugar-added strawberry pourable fruit*
4 tablespoons almond-flavored liqueur, divided**
1 cup heavy cream

2 tablespoons no-sugar-added strawberry fruit spread combined with 1 tablespoon warm water can be substituted.

**3 tablespoons thawed frozen unsweetened apple juice concentrate plus ½ teaspoon almond extract can be substituted for the liqueur in the berry mixture, and 1 tablespoon thawed frozen unsweetened apple juice concentrate can be substituted for the liqueur in the whipped cream mixture.*

1. Preheat oven to 425°F. Combine flour, baking powder and salt in medium bowl. Cut in butter with pastry blender or two knives until mixture resembles coarse crumbs. Add milk and vanilla; mix just until dry ingredients are moistened. Knead dough gently on lightly floured surface ten times. Roll or pat out to ½-inch thickness. Cut with 3-inch heart- or round-shaped biscuit cutter; place on ungreased baking sheet. If necessary, reroll scraps of dough in order to make six shortcakes. Beat egg and water in small bowl; brush lightly over dough. Bake 12 to 14 minutes or until golden brown. Cool slightly on wire rack.

2. Meanwhile, combine berries, pourable fruit and 3 tablespoons liqueur; let stand at room temperature 15 minutes. Beat cream with remaining 1 tablespoon liqueur until soft peaks form. Split warm shortcakes; fill with about ⅔ of the berry mixture and whipped cream. Replace tops of shortcakes; top with remaining berry mixture and whipped cream.
Makes 6 servings

Berry Shortcake

Chocolate Orange Marble Chiffon Cake

⅓ cup HERSHEY'S Cocoa
¼ cup hot water
3 tablespoons plus 1½ cups sugar, divided
2 tablespoons plus ½ cup vegetable oil, divided
2¼ cups all-purpose flour
1 tablespoon baking powder
1 teaspoon salt
¾ cup cold water
7 egg yolks
1 cup egg whites (about 8)
½ teaspoon cream of tartar
1 tablespoon freshly grated orange peel
Orange Glaze (page 206)

1. Remove top oven rack; move other rack to lowest position. Heat oven to 325°F.

2. Stir together cocoa and hot water in medium bowl. Stir in 3 tablespoons sugar and 2 tablespoons oil; set aside. Stir together flour, remaining 1½ cups sugar, baking powder and salt in large bowl. Add cold water, remaining ½ cup oil and egg yolks; beat with spoon until smooth.

3. Beat egg whites and cream of tartar in another large bowl on high speed of mixer until stiff peaks form. Pour egg yolk mixture in a thin stream over egg white mixture, gently folding just until blended. Remove 2 cups batter; add to chocolate mixture, gently folding until well blended. Fold orange peel into remaining batter.

4. Spoon half the orange batter into ungreased 10-inch tube pan; drop half the chocolate batter on top by spoonfuls. Repeat layers of orange and chocolate batters. Gently swirl with knife for marbled effect, leaving definite orange and chocolate areas.

5. Bake 1 hour and 15 to 20 minutes or until top springs back when lightly touched. Immediately invert cake onto heatproof funnel; cool cake completely. Remove cake from pan; invert onto serving plate. Prepare Orange Glaze; spread over top of cake, allowing glaze to run down sides. Garnish as desired.   *Makes 12 to 16 servings*

continued on page 206

Chocolate Orange Marble Chiffon Cake

Chocolate Orange Marble Chiffon Cake, continued

Orange Glaze

⅓ cup butter or margarine
2 cups powdered sugar
2 tablespoons orange juice
½ teaspoon freshly grated orange peel

Melt butter in medium saucepan over low heat. Remove from heat; gradually stir in powdered sugar, orange juice and orange peel, beating until smooth and of desired consistency. Add additional orange juice, 1 teaspoon at a time, if needed.

Makes about 1½ cups glaze

Apple and Walnut Strudel

1 package (about 17 ounces) frozen puff pastry
1 cup sour cream
1 egg, separated
1 tablespoon water
1 can (21 ounces) apple pie filling
1 cup coarsely chopped walnuts

1. Thaw puff pastry according to package directions.

2. Preheat oven to 375°F. Spray 2 baking sheets with nonstick cooking spray.

3. Combine sour cream and egg yolk in small bowl; set aside. In separate small bowl, mix egg white and water; set aside.

4. On lightly floured surface, roll 1 sheet pastry into 12×10-inch rectangle. Spread ½ of apple pie filling down center ⅓ of pastry. Spread ½ cup sour cream mixture over filling; sprinkle with ½ cup walnuts.

5. Fold one long side of pastry over filling mixture; fold other side over filling mixture, overlapping edges. Press edges together to seal. Place on baking sheet, seam side down, tucking under ends. Using sharp knife, make 7 diagonal slits on top; brush with egg white mixture. Repeat with remaining pastry, apple pie filling, sour cream mixture and walnuts. Bake 30 to 35 minutes or until golden brown. *Makes 16 servings*

Traditional Ricotta Cheesecake

Crust
- 1 cup finely crushed graham crackers
- ¼ cup sugar
- ¼ cup melted margarine

Filling
- 2 cups (15 ounces) **SARGENTO®** Light Ricotta Cheese
- ½ cup sugar
- ½ cup half-and-half
- 2 tablespoons all-purpose flour
- 1 tablespoon fresh lemon juice
- 1 teaspoon finely grated lemon peel
- ¼ teaspoon salt
- 2 eggs

Topping
- 1 cup light sour cream
- 2 tablespoons sugar
- 1 teaspoon vanilla

Combine graham crackers, ¼ cup sugar and margarine; mix well. Press evenly over bottom and 1½ inches up side of 8- or 9-inch springform pan. Refrigerate while preparing filling.

In bowl of electric mixer, combine ricotta cheese, ½ cup sugar, half and-half, flour, lemon juice, lemon peel and salt; blend until smooth. Add eggs, one at a time; blend until smooth. Pour into crust. Bake at 350°F 50 minutes or until center is just set. Remove from oven.

Beat sour cream with 2 tablespoons sugar and vanilla. Gently spoon onto warm cheesecake; spread evenly over surface. Return to oven 10 minutes. Turn off oven; cool in oven with door propped open 30 minutes. Remove to wire cooling rack; cool completely. Refrigerate at least 3 hours.   *Makes 8 servings*

decadent bars & brownies

Razz-Ma-Tazz Bars

½ cup (1 stick) butter or margarine
2 cups (12-ounce package) NESTLÉ® TOLL HOUSE® Premier White Morsels, *divided*
2 eggs
½ cup granulated sugar
1 cup all-purpose flour
½ teaspoon salt
½ teaspoon almond extract
½ cup seedless raspberry jam
¼ cup toasted sliced almonds

PREHEAT oven to 325°F. Grease and sugar 9-inch square baking pan.

MELT butter in medium, microwave-safe bowl on HIGH (100%) power for 1 minute; stir. Add *1 cup* morsels; let stand. Do not stir.

BEAT eggs in large mixer bowl until foamy. Add sugar; beat until light lemon colored, about 5 minutes. Stir in morsel-butter mixture. Add flour, salt and almond extract; mix at low speed until combined. Spread ⅔ of batter into prepared pan.

BAKE for 15 to 17 minutes or until light golden brown around edges. Remove from oven to wire rack.

HEAT jam in small, microwave-safe bowl on HIGH (100%) power for 30 seconds; stir. Spread jam over warm crust. Stir *remaining* morsels into *remaining* batter. Drop spoonfuls of batter over jam. Sprinkle with almonds.

BAKE for 25 to 30 minutes or until edges are browned. Cool completely in pan on wire rack. Cut into bars. *Makes 16 bars*

Razz-Ma-Tazz Bars

Hershey's White Chip Brownies

4 eggs
1¼ cups sugar
½ cup (1 stick) butter or margarine, melted
2 teaspoons vanilla extract
1⅓ cups all-purpose flour
⅔ cup HERSHEY'S Cocoa
1 teaspoon baking powder
½ teaspoon salt
2 cups (12-ounce package) HERSHEY'S Premier White Chips

1. Heat oven to 350°F. Grease 13×9×2-inch baking pan.

2. Beat eggs in large bowl until foamy; gradually beat in sugar. Add butter and vanilla; beat until blended. Stir together flour, cocoa, baking powder and salt; add to egg mixture, beating until blended. Stir in white chips. Spread batter into prepared pan.

3. Bake 25 to 30 minutes or until brownies begin to pull away from sides of pan. Cool completely in pan on wire rack. Cut into squares.   *Makes about 36 brownies*

Apple Crumb Squares

2 cups QUAKER® Oats (quick or old fashioned, uncooked)
1½ cups all-purpose flour
1 cup packed brown sugar
¾ cup (1½ sticks) butter or margarine, melted
1 teaspoon ground cinnamon
½ teaspoon baking soda
½ teaspoon salt (optional)
¼ teaspoon ground nutmeg
1 cup applesauce
½ cup chopped nuts

Preheat oven to 350°F. In large bowl, combine all ingredients except applesauce and nuts; mix until crumbly. Reserve 1 cup oats mixture. Press remaining mixture on bottom of greased 13×9-inch metal baking pan. Bake 13 to 15 minutes; cool. Spread applesauce over partially baked crust. Sprinkle reserved 1 cup oats mixture over top; sprinkle with nuts. Bake 13 to 15 minutes or until golden brown. Cool in pan on wire rack; cut into 2-inch squares.   *Makes about 2 dozen bars*

Hershey's White Chip Brownies

Pecan Pie Bars

　¾ **cup (1½ sticks) butter**
　½ **cup powdered sugar**
1½ **cups all-purpose flour**
　3 **eggs**
　2 **cups coarsely chopped pecans**
　1 **cup** *each* **granulated sugar and light corn syrup**
　2 **tablespoons melted butter**
　1 **teaspoon vanilla**

Preheat oven to 350°F. Beat ¾ cup butter and powdered sugar in large bowl until well blended. Add flour gradually, beating after each addition. (Mixture will be crumbly but press together easily.) Press dough evenly into ungreased 13×9-inch baking pan. Press mixture slightly up sides of pan (less than ¼ inch) to form lip to hold filling. Bake 20 to 25 minutes or until golden brown. Meanwhile, for filling, beat eggs in medium bowl. Add pecans, granulated sugar, corn syrup, 2 tablespoons melted butter and vanilla; mix well. Pour filling over partially baked crust. Return to oven; bake 35 to 40 minutes or until filling is set. Loosen edges with knife. Cool completely on wire rack before cutting into squares. Cover and refrigerate until 10 to 15 minutes before serving. *Do not freeze.* 　　*Makes about 4 dozen bars*

White Chocolate & Almond Brownies

½ **cup (1 stick) unsalted butter, melted**
8 **ounces white chocolate, melted**
3 **eggs, lightly beaten**
¾ **cup sugar**
1 **cup all-purpose flour**
1 **teaspoon vanilla**
¼ **teaspoon salt**
½ **cup slivered almonds**

Preheat oven to 325°F. Grease 9-inch square baking pan. Mix butter and white chocolate in small bowl. Mix eggs and sugar in large bowl; beat 2 to 3 minutes or until pale yellow. Beat in chocolate mixture, flour, vanilla and salt until smooth. Pour into prepared pan; sprinkle with almonds. Bake 35 to 40 minutes or until center is completely set. If necessary, cover pan loosely with foil during last 10 minutes of baking to prevent overbrowning. Cool completely in pan on wire rack. 　　*Makes 16 brownies*

Pecan Pie Bars

Caramel Fudge Brownies

1 jar (12 ounces) caramel ice cream topping
1¼ cups all-purpose flour, divided
¼ teaspoon baking powder
Dash salt
4 squares (1 ounce each) unsweetened chocolate, coarsely chopped
¾ cup (1½ sticks) butter
2 cups sugar
3 eggs
2 teaspoons vanilla
¾ cup semisweet chocolate chips
¾ cup chopped pecans

1. Preheat oven to 350°F. Lightly grease 13×9-inch baking pan.

2. Combine caramel topping and ¼ cup flour in small bowl; set aside. Combine remaining 1 cup flour, baking powder and salt in small bowl; mix well.

3. Place unsweetened chocolate and butter in medium microwavable bowl. Microwave at HIGH 2 minutes or until butter is melted; stir until chocolate is completely melted.

4. Stir sugar into melted chocolate. Add eggs and vanilla; stir until blended. Add flour mixture; stir until well blended. Spread chocolate mixture evenly in prepared pan.

5. Bake 25 minutes. Remove from oven; immediately spread caramel mixture over brownies. Sprinkle top evenly with chocolate chips and pecans.

6. Return pan to oven; bake 20 to 25 minutes or until topping is golden brown and bubbling. *Do not overbake.* Cool brownies completely in pan on wire rack. Cut into 2×1½-inch bars.   *Makes 3 dozen brownies*

tip

Pecans, a member of the hickory family, are native to the United States. They can be stored in an airtight container up to 3 months in the refrigerator and up to 6 months in the freezer.

Caramel Fudge Brownies

Lemon Bars

Crust
- 2 cups all-purpose flour
- ½ cup powdered sugar
- 1 cup (2 sticks) butter or margarine, softened

Filling
- 1 can (14 ounces) NESTLÉ® CARNATION® Sweetened Condensed Milk
- 4 eggs
- ⅔ cup lemon juice
- 1 tablespoon all-purpose flour
- 1 teaspoon baking powder
- ¼ teaspoon salt
- 4 drops yellow food coloring (optional)
- 1 tablespoon grated lemon peel
- Sifted powdered sugar (optional)

PREHEAT oven to 350°F.

For Crust

COMBINE flour and sugar in medium bowl. Cut in butter with pastry blender or two knives until mixture is crumbly. Press lightly onto bottom and halfway up sides of ungreased 13×9-inch baking pan.

BAKE for 20 minutes.

For Filling

BEAT sweetened condensed milk and eggs in large mixer bowl until fluffy. Beat in lemon juice, flour, baking powder, salt and food coloring just until blended. Fold in lemon peel; pour over crust.

BAKE for 20 to 25 minutes or until filling is set and crust is golden brown. Cool in pan on wire rack. Refrigerate for about 2 hours. Cut into bars; sprinkle with powdered sugar.

Makes 4 dozen bars

Lemon Bars

Almond-Orange Shortbread

1 cup (4 ounces) sliced almonds, divided
2 cups all-purpose flour
1 cup (2 sticks) cold butter, cut into pieces
½ cup *each* sugar and cornstarch
2 tablespoons grated orange peel
1 teaspoon almond extract

Preheat oven to 350°F. Spread ¾ cup almonds in single layer in ungreased baking pan. Bake 6 minutes or until golden, stirring often. Cool. *Reduce oven temperature to 325°F.* Place toasted almonds in food processor. Process using on/off pulses until coarsely chopped. Add flour, butter, sugar, cornstarch, peel and extract. Process using on/off pulses until mixture resembles coarse crumbs. Press dough evenly into 10×8¾-inch rectangle on large ungreased baking sheet. Score dough into 1¼-inch squares. Press 1 slice of remaining almonds on each square. Bake 30 to 40 minutes or until firm when pressed and lightly browned. Immediately cut along score lines. Remove to wire racks; cool completely. *Makes 4½ dozen cookies*

Spiced Date Bars

½ cup margarine, softened
1 cup packed brown sugar
2 eggs
¾ cup light sour cream
2 cups all-purpose flour
1 teaspoon *each* baking soda and ground cinnamon
½ teaspoon ground nutmeg
1 package (8 ounces) DOLE® Chopped Dates or Pitted Dates, chopped
Powdered sugar (optional)

• Beat margarine and brown sugar until light and fluffy. Beat in eggs, one at a time. Stir in sour cream.

• Combine dry ingredients. Beat into sour cream mixture; stir in dates. Spread batter evenly into greased 13×9-inch baking pan.

• Bake at 350°F 25 to 30 minutes or until toothpick inserted in center comes out clean. Cool completely in pan on wire rack. Cut into bars. Dust with powdered sugar. *Makes 24 bars*

Almond-Orange Shortbread

Marbled Cherry Brownies

Cherry Cream Filling (recipe follows)
½ **cup (1 stick) butter or margarine, melted**
⅓ **cup HERSHEY'S Cocoa**
2 **eggs**
1 **cup sugar**
1 **teaspoon vanilla extract**
½ **cup all-purpose flour**
½ **teaspoon baking powder**
¼ **teaspoon salt**

1. Prepare Cherry Cream Filling; set aside. Heat oven to 350°F. Grease 9-inch square baking pan.

2. Stir butter and cocoa in small bowl until well blended. Beat eggs in medium bowl until foamy. Gradually add sugar and vanilla, beating until well blended. Stir together flour, baking powder and salt; add to egg mixture. Add cocoa mixture; stir until well blended.

3. Spread half of chocolate batter into prepared pan; cover with cherry filling. Drop spoonfuls of remaining chocolate batter over filling. With knife or spatula, gently swirl chocolate batter into filling for marbled effect.

4. Bake 35 to 40 minutes or until brownies begin to pull away from sides of pan. Cool; cut into squares. Cover; refrigerate leftover brownies. Bring to room temperature to serve. *Makes about 16 brownies*

Cherry Cream Filling

1 **package (3 ounces) cream cheese, softened**
¼ **cup sugar**
1 **egg**
½ **teaspoon vanilla extract**
¼ **teaspoon almond extract**
⅓ **cup chopped maraschino cherries, well drained**
1 **to 2 drops red food color (optional)**

1. Beat cream cheese and sugar in small bowl on medium speed of mixer until blended. Add egg, vanilla and almond extract; beat well. (Mixture will be thin.)

2. Stir in cherries and food color, if desired.

Marbled Cherry Brownies

Chocolate & Malt Bars

   1 cup all-purpose flour
   1 cup malted milk powder or malted milk drink mix
   2 teaspoons baking powder
   ¼ teaspoon salt
   ½ cup granulated sugar
   ¼ cup firmly packed light brown sugar
   ¼ cup (½ stick) butter, softened
   ½ cup milk
   ½ teaspoon vanilla extract
   2 eggs
   1 cup "M&M's"® Chocolate Mini Baking Bits, divided
      Chocolate Malt Frosting (recipe follows)

Preheat oven to 350°F. Lightly grease 13×9-inch baking pan; set aside. In large bowl combine flour, malted milk powder, baking powder and salt; stir in sugars. Beat in butter, milk and vanilla; blend well. Add eggs; beat 2 minutes. Spread batter in prepared pan. Sprinkle with ¼ cup "M&M's"® Chocolate Mini Baking Bits. Bake about 20 minutes or until toothpick inserted in center comes out clean. Cool completely on wire rack. Prepare Chocolate Malt Frosting; spread over cake. Sprinkle with remaining ¾ cup "M&M's"® Chocolate Mini Baking Bits. Store in tightly covered container.   *Makes 2 dozen bars*

Chocolate Malt Frosting

   ¼ cup (½ stick) butter, softened
   4 teaspoons light corn syrup
   ½ teaspoon vanilla extract
   3 tablespoons unsweetened cocoa powder
   ¼ cup malted milk powder or malted milk drink mix
 1½ cups powdered sugar
   3 to 4 tablespoons milk

In small bowl beat butter, corn syrup and vanilla; add cocoa powder and malted milk powder until well blended. Blend in powdered sugar and enough milk for good spreading consistency.

Chocolate & Malt Bars

Fruit and Oat Squares

1 cup *each* **all-purpose flour and uncooked quick oats**
¾ cup packed light brown sugar
½ teaspoon baking soda
¼ teaspoon *each* **salt and ground cinnamon**
⅓ cup butter, melted
¾ cup apricot, cherry or other fruit flavor preserves

Preheat oven to 350°F. Lightly grease 9-inch square baking pan; set aside. Combine flour, oats, brown sugar, baking soda, salt and cinnamon in medium bowl; mix well. Add butter; stir with fork until mixture is crumbly. Reserve ¾ cup crumb mixture for topping. Press remaining crumb mixture evenly onto bottom of prepared pan. Bake 5 to 7 minutes or until lightly browned. Spread preserves onto crust; sprinkle with reserved crumb mixture. Bake 20 to 25 minutes or until golden brown. Cool completely in pan on wire rack. Cut into 16 squares.   *Makes 16 squares*

Chewy Butterscotch Brownies

2½ cups all-purpose flour
1 teaspoon baking powder
½ teaspoon salt
1 cup (2 sticks) butter or margarine, softened
1¾ cups packed brown sugar
1 tablespoon vanilla extract
2 eggs
**1⅔ cups (11-ounce package) NESTLÉ® TOLL HOUSE® Butterscotch
    Flavored Morsels,** *divided*
1 cup chopped nuts

PREHEAT oven to 350°F.

COMBINE flour, baking powder and salt in medium bowl. Beat butter, sugar and vanilla extract in large mixer bowl until creamy. Beat in eggs. Gradually beat in flour mixture. Stir in *1 cup* morsels and nuts. Spread into ungreased 13×9-inch baking pan. Sprinkle with *remaining* morsels.

BAKE for 30 to 40 minutes or until wooden pick inserted in center comes out clean. Cool in pan on wire rack. Cut into bars.   *Makes about 4 dozen brownies*

Fruit and Oat Squares

Reese's® Peanut Butter and Milk Chocolate Chip Brownies

¾ cup HERSHEY'S® Cocoa
½ teaspoon baking soda
⅔ cup butter or margarine, melted and divided
½ cup boiling water
2 cups sugar
2 eggs
1⅓ cups all-purpose flour
1 teaspoon vanilla extract
¼ teaspoon salt
1¾ cups (11-ounce package) REESE'S® Peanut Butter and Milk Chocolate Chips

1. Heat oven to 350°F. Grease 13×9×2-inch baking pan.

2. Stir together cocoa and baking soda in large bowl; stir in ⅓ cup butter. Add boiling water; stir until mixture thickens. Stir in sugar, eggs and remaining ⅓ cup butter; stir until smooth. Add flour, vanilla and salt; blend completely. Stir in chips. Pour into prepared pan.

3. Bake 35 to 40 minutes or until brownies begin to pull away from sides of pan. Cool completely in pan on wire rack. Cut into squares.   *Makes about 36 brownies*

tip

For easy removal of brownies and bar cookies (and no cleanup!), line the baking pan with foil and leave at least 3 inches hanging over each end. Use the foil to lift out the treats, place them on a cutting board and carefully remove the foil. Then simply cut them into bars or squares.

Reese's® Peanut Butter and Milk Chocolate Chip Brownies

Oatmeal Toffee Bars

1 cup (2 sticks) butter or margarine, softened
1 cup packed light brown sugar
2 eggs
1 teaspoon vanilla extract
1½ cups all-purpose flour
1 teaspoon baking soda
½ teaspoon ground cinnamon
½ teaspoon salt
1⅓ cups (8-ounce package) HEATH® BITS 'O BRICKLE® Toffee Bits, divided
3 cups quick-cooking or regular rolled oats

1. Heat oven to 350°F. Grease 13×9×2-inch baking pan.

2. Beat butter and brown sugar in large bowl until well blended. Add eggs and vanilla; beat well. Stir together flour, baking soda, cinnamon and salt; gradually add to butter mixture, beating until well blended. Set aside ¼ cup toffee bits. Stir remaining toffee bits and oats into batter (batter will be stiff). Spread batter into prepared pan; sprinkle reserved ¼ cup toffee bits over surface.

3. Bake 25 minutes or until wooden pick inserted in center comes out clean. Cool completely in pan on wire rack. Cut into bars. *Makes about 36 bars*

Hint: Bar cookies can be cut into different shapes for variety. To cut into triangles, cut cookie bars into 2- to 3-inch squares, then diagonally cut each square in half. To make diamond shapes, cut parallel lines 2 inches apart across the length of the pan, then cut diagonal lines 2 inches apart.

Oatmeal Toffee Bars

Peanutty Cranberry Bars

½ **cup (1 stick) butter or margarine, softened**
½ **cup granulated sugar**
¼ **cup packed light brown sugar**
 1 **cup all-purpose flour**
 1 **cup quick-cooking rolled oats**
¼ **teaspoon baking soda**
¼ **teaspoon salt**
 1 **cup REESE'S® Peanut Butter Chips**
1½ **cups fresh or frozen whole cranberries**
⅔ **cup light corn syrup**
½ **cup water**
 1 **teaspoon vanilla extract**

1. Heat oven to 350°F. Grease 8-inch square baking pan.

2. Beat butter, granulated sugar and brown sugar in medium bowl until fluffy. Stir together flour, oats, baking soda and salt; gradually add to butter mixture, mixing until mixture is consistency of coarse crumbs. Stir in peanut butter chips.

3. Reserve 1½ cups mixture for crumb topping. Firmly press remaining mixture evenly into prepared pan. Bake 15 minutes or until set. Meanwhile, in medium saucepan, combine cranberries, corn syrup and water. Cook over medium heat, stirring occasionally, until mixture boils. Reduce heat; simmer 15 minutes, stirring occasionally. Remove from heat. Stir in vanilla. Spread evenly over baked layer. Sprinkle reserved 1½ cups crumbs evenly over top.

4. Return to oven. Bake 15 to 20 minutes or until set. Cool completely in pan on wire rack. Cut into bars. *Makes about 16 bars*

Peanutty Cranberry Bars

Cheesecake-Topped Brownies

1 (21.5- or 23.6-ounce) package fudge brownie mix
1 (8-ounce) package cream cheese, softened
2 tablespoons butter or margarine, softened
1 tablespoon cornstarch
1 (14-ounce) can EAGLE BRAND® Sweetened Condensed Milk
    (NOT evaporated milk)
1 egg
2 teaspoons vanilla extract
    Ready-to-spread chocolate frosting, if desired
    Orange peel, if desired

1. Preheat oven to 350°F. Prepare brownie mix as package directs. Spread into well-greased 13×9-inch baking pan.

2. In large mixing bowl, beat cream cheese, butter and cornstarch until fluffy.

3. Gradually beat in Eagle Brand. Add egg and vanilla; beat until smooth. Pour cheesecake mixture evenly over brownie batter.

4. Bake 40 to 45 minutes or until top is lightly browned. Cool. Spread with frosting or sprinkle with orange peel, if desired. Cut into bars. Store covered in refrigerator.

Makes 3 to 3½ dozen brownies

Prep Time: 20 minutes
Bake Time: 40 to 45 minutes

Cheesecake-Topped Brownies

Chocolate Toffee Gems

2½ cups all-purpose flour
1½ teaspoons baking soda
¾ teaspoon salt
1 cup (2 sticks) unsalted butter, softened
¾ cup firmly packed light brown sugar
⅓ cup granulated sugar
2 eggs, lightly beaten
2 teaspoons vanilla
1 package (10 ounces) toffee baking pieces
½ cup sweetened condensed milk (not evaporated milk)
1½ cups semisweet chocolate chips

1. Preheat oven to 350°F. Grease 13×9-inch baking pan. Sift together flour, baking soda and salt in medium bowl; set aside.

2. Beat butter and sugars in large bowl at medium speed of electric mixer until creamy. Add eggs and vanilla; beat until smooth. Gradually stir in flour mixture. Reserve ¼ cup toffee baking pieces for garnish. Stir in remaining toffee pieces. Spread mixture in prepared baking pan. Bake 35 to 40 minutes. Cool completely in pan on wire rack.

3. Combine sweetened condensed milk and chocolate chips in small saucepan. Cook and stir over low heat until chips are melted. Spread chocolate mixture over bars; sprinkle with reserved toffee pieces. Let stand until topping is set; cut into 1-inch squares.

Makes about 3 dozen squares

tip

Sweetened condensed milk is a canned product that is the result of evaporating about half of the water from whole milk and adding cane sugar or corn syrup to sweeten and preserve the milk. It is used for desserts and candy and should not be confused with evaporated milk. Unopened cans of sweetened condensed milk can be stored at room temperature for up to 6 months.

Chocolate Toffee Gems

Swirled Peanut Butter Chocolate Cheesecake Bars

Crust
>   2 cups graham cracker crumbs
>   ½ cup (1 stick) butter or margarine, melted
>   ⅓ cup granulated sugar

Filling
>   2 packages (8 ounces *each*) cream cheese, softened
>   1 cup granulated sugar
>   ¼ cup all-purpose flour
>   1 can (12 fluid ounces) NESTLÉ® CARNATION® Evaporated Milk
>   2 eggs
>   1 tablespoon vanilla extract
>   1 cup (6 ounces) NESTLÉ® TOLL HOUSE® Peanut Butter & Milk
>   Chocolate Morsels

PREHEAT oven to 325°F.

For Crust

COMBINE graham cracker crumbs, butter and sugar in medium bowl; press onto bottom of ungreased 13×9-inch baking pan.

For Filling

BEAT cream cheese, sugar and flour in large mixer bowl until smooth. Gradually beat in evaporated milk, eggs and vanilla extract.

MICROWAVE morsels in medium, uncovered, microwave-safe bowl on MEDIUM–HIGH (70%) power for 1 minute. STIR. Morsels may retain some of their original shape. If necessary, microwave at additional 10- to 15-second intervals, stirring just until morsels are melted. Stir *1 cup* cream cheese mixture into chocolate. Pour *remaining* cream cheese mixture over crust. Pour chocolate mixture over cream cheese mixture. Swirl mixtures with spoon, pulling plain cream cheese mixture up to surface.

BAKE for 40 to 45 minutes or until set. Cool completely in pan on wire rack; refrigerate until firm. Cut into bars.   *Makes 15 bars*

Swirled Peanut Butter Chocolate Cheesecake Bars

Chocolate Almond Macaroon Bars

2 cups chocolate wafer cookie crumbs
6 tablespoons butter or margarine, melted
6 tablespoons powdered sugar
1 can (14 ounces) sweetened condensed milk
3¾ cups (10-ounce package) MOUNDS™ Sweetened Coconut Flakes
1 cup sliced almonds, toasted* (optional)
1 cup HERSHEY'S Semi-Sweet Chocolate Chips
¼ cup whipping cream
½ cup HERSHEY'S Premier White Chips

*To toast almonds: heat oven to 350°F. Spread almonds evenly on shallow baking sheet. Bake 5 to 8 minutes or until lightly browned.

1. Heat oven to 350°F. Grease 13×9×2-inch baking pan.

2. Combine crumbs, melted butter and sugar in large bowl. Firmly press crumb mixture on bottom of prepared pan. Stir together sweetened condensed milk, coconut and almonds in large bowl, mixing well. Carefully drop mixture by spoonfuls over crust; spread evenly.

3. Bake 20 to 25 minutes or until coconut edges just begin to brown. Cool.

4. Place chocolate chips and whipping cream in medium microwave-safe bowl. Microwave at HIGH (100% power) 1 minute; stir. If necessary, microwave at HIGH an additional 10 seconds at a time, stirring after each heating, until chips are melted and mixture is smooth when stirred. Cool until slightly thickened; spread over cooled bars. Sprinkle top with white chips. Cover; refrigerate several hours or until thoroughly chilled. Cut into bars. Refrigerate leftovers.   *Makes about 36 bars*

Chocolate Almond Macaroon Bars

irresistible cookies & treats

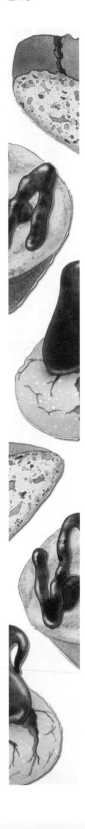

Oatmeal Scotchies

1 ¼ cups all-purpose flour
1 teaspoon baking soda
½ teaspoon salt
½ teaspoon ground cinnamon
1 cup (2 sticks) butter or margarine, softened
¾ cup granulated sugar
¾ cup packed brown sugar
2 eggs
1 teaspoon vanilla extract *or* grated peel of 1 orange
3 cups quick or old-fashioned oats
1 ⅔ cups (11-ounce package) NESTLÉ® TOLL HOUSE® Butterscotch Flavored Morsels

PREHEAT oven to 375°F.

COMBINE flour, baking soda, salt and cinnamon in small bowl. Beat butter, granulated sugar, brown sugar, eggs and vanilla extract in large mixer bowl. Gradually beat in flour mixture. Stir in oats and morsels. Drop by rounded tablespoon onto ungreased baking sheets.

BAKE for 7 to 8 minutes for chewy cookies or 9 to 10 minutes for crispy cookies. Cool on baking sheets for 2 minutes; remove to wire racks to cool completely.

Makes about 4 dozen cookies

Pan Cookie Variation: GREASE 15×10-inch jelly-roll pan. Spread dough into prepared pan. Bake for 18 to 22 minutes or until light brown. Cool completely in pan on wire rack. Makes 4 dozen bars.

Oatmeal Scotchies

Ultimate White & Dark Chocolate Chippers

        1 cup (2 sticks) butter, softened
    ¾ cup granulated sugar
    ¾ cup packed light brown sugar
        2 eggs
        2 tablespoons almond-flavored liqueur or water
        1 teaspoon baking soda
        1 teaspoon vanilla
    ¼ teaspoon salt
    2⅓ cups all-purpose flour
        1 cup (6 ounces) semisweet chocolate chips
        1 cup (6 ounces) white chocolate chips
        1 cup coarsely chopped pecans

1. Preheat oven to 375°F. Line cookie sheets with parchment paper or leave ungreased.

2. Combine butter, sugars, eggs, liqueur, baking soda, vanilla and salt in large bowl; beat until light and fluffy. Blend in flour until dough is smooth and stiff. Stir in chips and pecans.

3. Drop dough by teaspoonfuls 2 inches apart onto prepared cookie sheets. Bake 8 to 10 minutes or until just firm in center and edges are lightly browned. Do not overbake. Remove to wire racks; cool completely.   *Makes about 5 dozen cookies*

Ultimate White & Dark Chocolate Chippers

Banana Sandies

2⅓ cups all-purpose flour
1 cup (2 sticks) butter, softened
¾ cup granulated sugar
¼ cup packed light brown sugar
½ cup ¼-inch slices banana (about 1 medium)
1 teaspoon vanilla
¼ teaspoon salt
⅔ cup chopped pecans
Prepared cream cheese frosting
Yellow food coloring (optional)

1. Preheat oven to 350°F. Grease cookie sheets.

2. Combine flour, butter, sugars, banana, vanilla and salt in large bowl. Beat 2 to 3 minutes, scraping bowl often, until well blended. Stir in pecans. Shape dough by rounded teaspoonfuls into 1-inch balls. Place 2 inches apart on prepared cookie sheets; flatten to ¼-inch thickness with bottom of glass dipped in sugar. Bake 12 to 15 minutes or until edges are lightly browned. Remove immediately to wire racks; cool completely.

3. Tint frosting with food coloring, if desired. Spread 1 tablespoon frosting over bottoms of half the cookies. Top with remaining cookies.

Makes about 2 dozen sandwich cookies

tip

To soften butter for use in batters and doughs, place 1 unwrapped stick on a microwavable plate and heat at LOW (30% power) about 30 seconds or just until softened.

Banana Sandies

Reese's® Peanut Butter and Milk Chocolate Chip Tassies

¾ **cup (1½ sticks) butter, softened**
1 **package (3 ounces) cream cheese, softened**
1½ **cups all-purpose flour**
¾ **cup sugar, divided**
1 **egg, slightly beaten**
2 **tablespoons butter or margarine, melted**
¼ **teaspoon lemon juice**
¼ **teaspoon vanilla extract**
1¾ **cups (11-ounce package) REESE'S® Peanut Butter and Milk**
   Chocolate Chips, divided
2 **teaspoons shortening (do not use butter, margarine, spread or oil)**

1. Beat ¾ cup butter and cream cheese in medium bowl; add flour and ¼ cup sugar, beating until well blended. Cover; refrigerate about 1 hour or until dough is firm. Shape dough into 1-inch balls; press balls onto bottoms and up sides of about 36 small muffin cups (1¾ inches in diameter).

2. Heat oven to 350°F. Combine egg, remaining ½ cup sugar, melted butter, lemon juice and vanilla in small bowl; stir until smooth. Set aside ⅓ cup chips; add remainder to egg mixture. Evenly fill muffin cups with chip mixture.

3. Bake 20 to 25 minutes or until filling is set and lightly browned. Cool completely; remove from pan to wire rack.

4. Combine reserved ⅓ cup chips and shortening in small microwave-safe bowl. Microwave at HIGH (100% power) 30 seconds; stir. If necessary, microwave additional 15 seconds at a time, stirring after each heating, until chips are melted and mixture is smooth when stirred. Drizzle over tops of tassies.

Makes 3 dozen cookies

Reese's® Peanut Butter and Milk Chocolate Chip Tassies

Jumbo 3-Chip Cookies

    4 cups all-purpose flour
    1 teaspoon baking powder
    1 teaspoon baking soda
 1½ cups (3 sticks) butter, softened
 1¼ cups granulated sugar
 1¼ cups packed brown sugar
    2 eggs
    1 tablespoon vanilla extract
    1 cup (6 ounces) NESTLÉ® TOLL HOUSE® Milk Chocolate Morsels
    1 cup (6 ounces) NESTLÉ® TOLL HOUSE® Semi-Sweet Chocolate
       Morsels
 ½ cup NESTLÉ® TOLL HOUSE® Premier White Morsels
    1 cup chopped nuts

PREHEAT oven to 375°F.

COMBINE flour, baking powder and baking soda in medium bowl. Beat butter, granulated sugar and brown sugar in large mixer bowl until creamy. Beat in eggs and vanilla extract. Gradually beat in flour mixture. Stir in morsels and nuts. Drop dough by level ¼ cup measure 2 inches apart onto ungreased baking sheets.

BAKE for 12 to 14 minutes or until light golden brown. Cool on baking sheets for 2 minutes; remove to wire racks to cool completely.

Makes about 2 dozen cookies

Jumbo 3-Chip Cookies

Tiny Mini Kisses Peanut Blossoms

¾ cup **REESE'S®** Creamy Peanut Butter
½ **cup shortening**
⅓ **cup granulated sugar**
⅓ **cup packed light brown sugar**
1 **egg**
3 **tablespoons milk**
1 **teaspoon vanilla extract**
1½ **cups all-purpose flour**
½ **teaspoon baking soda**
½ **teaspoon salt**
    Granulated sugar
    HERSHEY'S MINI KISSES™ Milk Chocolates

1. Heat oven to 350°F.

2. Beat peanut butter and shortening in large bowl with mixer until well blended. Add ⅓ cup granulated sugar and brown sugar; beat well. Add egg, milk and vanilla; beat until fluffy. Stir together flour, baking soda and salt; gradually add to peanut butter mixture, beating until blended. Shape into ½-inch balls. Roll in granulated sugar; place on ungreased cookie sheet.

3. Bake 5 to 6 minutes or until set. Immediately press Mini Kiss™ into center of each cookie. Remove from cookie sheet to wire rack.   *Makes about 14 dozen cookies*

Variation: For larger cookies, shape dough into 1-inch balls. Roll in granulated sugar. Place on ungreased cookie sheet. Bake 10 minutes or until set. Immediately place 3 Mini Kisses™ in center of each cookie, pressing down slightly. Remove from cookie sheet to wire rack. Cool completely.

Tiny Mini Kisses Peanut Blossoms

White Chip Apricot Oatmeal Cookies

¾ cup (1½ sticks) butter or margarine, softened
½ cup *each* granulated sugar and packed light brown sugar
1 egg
1 cup all-purpose flour
1 teaspoon baking soda
2½ cups rolled oats
1⅔ cups (10-ounce package) HERSHEY'S Premier White Chips
¾ cup chopped dried apricots

1. Heat oven to 375°F.

2. Beat butter, granulated sugar and brown sugar in large bowl until fluffy. Add egg; beat well. Add flour and baking soda; beat until well blended. Stir in oats, white chips and apricots. Loosely form rounded teaspoonfuls dough into balls; place on ungreased cookie sheet.

3. Bake 7 to 9 minutes or until lightly browned; do not overbake. Cool slightly; remove from cookie sheet to wire rack. Cool completely.   *Makes about 3½ dozen cookies*

Thumbprint Cookies

1 cup butter or margarine
¼ cup sugar
1 teaspoon almond extract
2 cups all-purpose flour
½ teaspoon salt
1 cup finely chopped nuts, if desired
SMUCKER'S® Preserves or Jams (any flavor)

1. Heat oven to 400°F. Place sheets of foil on countertop for cooling cookies.

2. Combine butter and sugar in large bowl. Beat until light and fluffy. Blend in almond extract. Add flour and salt; mix well.

3. Shape level tablespoonfuls of dough into balls; roll in nuts. Place on ungreased cookie sheets; flatten slightly. Indent centers; fill with preserves or jams.

4. Bake for 10 to 12 minutes or until lightly browned.   *Makes 2½ dozen cookies*

White Chip Apricot Oatmeal Cookies

Spicy Ginger Molasses Cookies

      2 cups all-purpose flour
1 ½ teaspoons ground ginger
      1 teaspoon baking soda
      ½ teaspoon ground cloves
      ¼ teaspoon salt
      ¾ cup (1 ½ sticks) butter, softened
      1 cup sugar
      ¼ cup molasses
      1 egg
         Additional sugar
      ½ cup yogurt-covered raisins

1. Preheat oven to 375°F. Line cookie sheets with parchment paper.

2. Combine flour, ginger, baking soda, cloves and salt in small bowl; set aside.

3. Beat butter and 1 cup sugar in large bowl at medium speed of electric mixer until light and fluffy. Add molasses and egg; beat until well blended. Gradually beat in flour mixture at low speed just until blended.

4. Drop dough by level ¼ cupfuls about 3 inches apart onto prepared cookie sheets. Flatten with bottom of glass dipped in additional sugar until about 2 inches in diameter. Press yogurt-covered raisins into dough.

5. Bake 11 to 12 minutes or until cookies are set. Cool 2 minutes on cookie sheets; slide parchment paper and cookies onto wire racks. Cool completely.

Makes about 1 dozen (4-inch) cookies

Spicy Ginger Molasses Cookies

Classic Anise Biscotti

4 ounces whole blanched almonds (about ¾ cup)
2¼ cups all-purpose flour
1 teaspoon baking powder
¾ teaspoon salt
¾ cup sugar
½ cup unsalted butter, softened
3 eggs
2 tablespoons brandy
2 teaspoons grated lemon peel
1 tablespoon whole anise seeds

1. Preheat oven to 375°F. To toast almonds, spread almonds on baking sheet. Bake 6 to 8 minutes or until toasted and light brown; turn off oven. Let almonds cool slightly; coarsely chop.

2. Combine flour, baking powder and salt in small bowl. Beat sugar and butter in medium bowl with electric mixer at medium speed until light and fluffy. Add eggs, 1 at a time, beating well after each addition and scraping side of bowl often. Stir in brandy and lemon peel. Add flour mixture gradually; stir until smooth. Stir in chopped almonds and anise seeds. Cover and refrigerate dough 1 hour or until firm.

3. Preheat oven to 375°F. Grease large baking sheet. Divide dough in half. Shape ½ of dough into 12×2-inch log on lightly floured surface. (Dough will be fairly soft.) Pat smooth with lightly floured fingertips. Transfer to prepared baking sheet. Repeat with remaining ½ of dough to form second log. Bake 20 to 25 minutes or until logs are light golden brown. Turn off oven. Cool logs completely on baking sheet on wire rack.

4. Preheat oven to 350°F. Cut logs diagonally with serrated knife into ½-inch-thick slices. Place slices flat in single layer on 2 ungreased baking sheets.

5. Bake 8 minutes. Turn slices over; bake 10 to 12 minutes or until cut surfaces are light brown and cookies are dry. Remove cookies to wire racks; cool completely. Store cookies in airtight container up to 2 weeks.   *Makes about 4 dozen cookies*

Classic Anise Biscotti

Lemon Coconut Pixies

¼ cup (½ stick) butter or margarine, softened
1 cup sugar
2 eggs
1½ teaspoons freshly grated lemon peel
1½ cups all-purpose flour
2 teaspoons baking powder
¼ teaspoon salt
1 cup MOUNDS™ Sweetened Coconut Flakes
Powdered sugar

1. Heat oven to 300°F.

2. Beat butter, sugar, eggs and lemon peel in large bowl until well blended. Stir together flour, baking powder and salt; gradually add to lemon mixture, beating until blended. Stir in coconut. Cover; refrigerate dough about 1 hour or until firm enough to handle. Shape into 1-inch balls; roll in powdered sugar. Place 2 inches apart on ungreased cookie sheet.

3. Bake 15 to 18 minutes or until edges are set. Immediately remove from cookie sheet to wire rack. Cool completely. Store in tightly covered container in cool, dry place. *Makes about 4 dozen cookies*

Lemon Coconut Pixies

Sour Cream Chocolate Chip Cookies

**1 Butter Flavor CRISCO® Stick or 1 cup Butter Flavor CRISCO®
all-vegetable shortening plus additional for greasing**
1 cup firmly packed light brown sugar
½ cup granulated sugar
1 egg
½ cup dairy sour cream
¼ cup warm honey
2 teaspoons vanilla
2½ cups all-purpose flour
1½ teaspoons baking powder
½ teaspoon salt
2 cups semisweet or milk chocolate chips
1 cup coarsely chopped walnuts

1. Heat oven to 375°F. Grease baking sheet. Place sheets of foil on countertop for cooling cookies.

2. Combine 1 cup shortening, brown sugar and granulated sugar in large bowl. Beat at medium speed of electric mixer until well blended. Beat in egg, sour cream, honey and vanilla. Beat until just blended.

3. Combine flour, baking powder and salt. Mix into creamed mixture at low speed until just blended. Stir in chocolate chips and nuts.

4. Drop slightly rounded measuring tablespoonfuls of dough 2 inches apart onto prepared baking sheet.

5. Bake at 375°F 10 to 12 minutes or until set. *Do not overbake.* Cool 2 minutes on baking sheet. Remove to foil to cool completely.   *Makes about 5 dozen cookies*

Butterscotch Thins

2⅔ cups all-purpose flour
1½ teaspoons baking soda
1⅔ cups (11-ounce package) NESTLÉ® TOLL HOUSE® Butterscotch
  Flavored Morsels
  1 cup (2 sticks) butter or margarine, cut into pieces
1⅓ cups packed brown sugar
  2 eggs
1½ teaspoons vanilla extract
  ⅔ cup finely chopped nuts

COMBINE flour and baking soda in medium bowl.

MICROWAVE morsels and butter in large, uncovered, microwave-safe mixer bowl on MEDIUM–HIGH (70%) power for 1 minute; STIR. The morsels may retain some of their original shape. If necessary, microwave at additional 10- to 15-second intervals, stirring just until smooth. Beat in brown sugar, eggs and vanilla extract. Gradually beat in flour mixture; stir in nuts. Cover; refrigerate for about 1 hour or until firm. Shape into two 14×1½-inch logs; wrap in plastic wrap. Refrigerate for 2 hours or until firm.

PREHEAT oven to 375°F.

UNWRAP logs; slice into ¼-inch-thick slices. Place slices on ungreased baking sheets.

BAKE for 5 to 6 minutes or until edges are set. Cool on baking sheets for 2 minutes; remove to wire racks to cool completely.   *Makes about 6 dozen cookies*

tip

Use gentle pressure and a back-and-forth sawing motion when slicing the cookie dough log. Rotating the log while slicing also prevents one side from becoming flat.

Cut-Out Sugar Cookies

1¼ cups granulated sugar
   1 Butter Flavor CRISCO® Stick or 1 cup Butter Flavor CRISCO®
      all-vegetable shortening
   2 eggs
¼ cup light corn syrup or regular pancake syrup
   1 tablespoon vanilla
   3 cups plus 4 tablespoons all-purpose flour, divided
¾ teaspoon baking powder
½ teaspoon baking soda
½ teaspoon salt
   Granulated sugar or colored sugar crystals

1. Combine sugar and 1 cup shortening in large bowl. Beat at medium speed of electric mixer until well blended. Add eggs, syrup and vanilla. Beat until well blended and fluffy.

2. Combine 3 cups flour, baking powder, baking soda and salt. Add gradually to shortening mixture at low speed. Mix until well blended.

3. Divide dough into 4 quarters. Wrap each quarter of dough with plastic wrap. Refrigerate at least 1 hour. Keep refrigerated until ready to use.

4. Heat oven to 375°F. Place sheets of foil on countertop for cooling cookies.

5. Sprinkle 1 tablespoon flour over large sheet of waxed paper. Place one quarter of dough on floured paper. Flatten slightly with hands. Turn dough over and cover with another large sheet of waxed paper. Roll dough to ¼-inch thickness. Remove top sheet of waxed paper. Cut out with floured cutters. Place 2 inches apart on ungreased baking sheets. Repeat with remaining dough.

6. Sprinkle cut-outs with granulated sugar or colored sugar crystals, or leave plain to frost or decorate when cooled.

7. Bake one baking sheet at a time at 375°F for 5 to 9 minutes, depending on size of cookies (bake smaller, thinner cookies closer to 5 minutes; larger cookies closer to 9 minutes). *Do not overbake.* Cool 2 minutes on baking sheets. Remove cookies to foil to cool completely, then frost and decorate, if desired.

Makes about 3 to 4 dozen cookies

Cut-Out Sugar Cookies

Chocolate Macadamia Chewies

> ¾ cup (1½ sticks) butter or margarine, softened
> ⅔ cup firmly packed light brown sugar
> 1 egg
> 1 teaspoon vanilla extract
> 1¾ cups all-purpose flour
> ¾ teaspoon baking soda
> ¼ teaspoon salt
> ¾ cup (3½ ounces) coarsely chopped macadamia nuts
> ½ cup shredded coconut
> 1¾ cups "M&M's"® Chocolate Mini Baking Bits

Preheat oven to 350°F. In large bowl cream butter and sugar until light and fluffy; beat in egg and vanilla. In medium bowl combine flour, baking soda and salt; blend into creamed mixture. Blend in nuts and coconut. Stir in "M&M's"® Chocolate Mini Baking Bits. Drop by heaping teaspoonfuls about 2 inches apart onto ungreased cookie sheets; flatten slightly with back of spoon. Bake 8 to 10 minutes or until set. Do not overbake. Cool 1 minute on cookie sheets; cool completely on wire racks. Store in tightly covered container. *Makes about 4 dozen cookies*

Coconut Macaroons

> 1 (14-ounce) can EAGLE BRAND® Sweetened Condensed Milk (NOT evaporated milk)
> 1 egg white
> 2 teaspoons vanilla extract
> 1 to 1½ teaspoons almond extract
> 2 (7-ounce) packages flaked coconut (5⅓ cups)

1. Preheat oven to 325°F. Line baking sheets with foil; grease and flour foil. Set aside.

2. In large mixing bowl, combine Eagle Brand, egg white, vanilla and almond extract. Stir in coconut. Drop by rounded teaspoonfuls onto prepared sheets; with spoon, slightly flatten each mound.

3. Bake 15 to 17 minutes or until golden. Remove from baking sheets; cool on wire racks. Store loosely covered at room temperature. *Makes about 4 dozen cookies*

Chocolate Macadamia Chewies

Anna's Icing Oatmeal Sandwich Cookies

Cookies
  ¾ **Butter Flavor CRISCO® Stick or ¾ cup Butter Flavor CRISCO®**
    all-vegetable shortening plus additional for greasing
1¼ **cups firmly packed light brown sugar**
  ⅓ **cup milk**
  1 **egg**
1½ **teaspoons vanilla**
  3 **cups quick oats, uncooked**
  1 **cup all-purpose flour**
  ½ **teaspoon baking soda**
  ½ **teaspoon salt**

Frosting
  2 **cups confectioners' sugar**
  ¼ **Butter Flavor CRISCO® Stick or ¼ cup Butter Flavor CRISCO®**
    all-vegetable shortening
  ½ **teaspoon vanilla**
    Milk

1. Heat oven to 350°F. Grease baking sheets with shortening. Place sheets of foil on countertop for cooling cookies.

2. For cookies, combine ¾ cup shortening, brown sugar, milk, egg and vanilla in large bowl. Beat at medium speed of electric mixer until well blended.

3. Combine oats, flour, baking soda and salt. Mix into creamed mixture at low speed just until blended.

4. Drop rounded measuring tablespoonfuls of dough 2 inches apart onto prepared baking sheets.

5. Bake one sheet at a time at 375°F for 10 to 12 minutes or until lightly browned. *Do not overbake.* Cool 2 minutes on baking sheet. Remove cookies to foil to cool completely.

6. For frosting, combine confectioners' sugar, ¼ cup shortening and vanilla in medium bowl. Beat at low speed, adding enough milk for good spreading consistency. Spread on bottoms of half the cookies. Top with remaining cookies.

Makes about 16 sandwich cookies

Anna's Icing Oatmeal Sandwich Cookies

Chocolate-Coconut-Toffee Delights

½ cup all-purpose flour
¼ teaspoon baking powder
¼ teaspoon salt
1 package (12 ounces) semisweet chocolate chips, divided
¼ cup (½ stick) butter, cut into small pieces
¾ cup packed light brown sugar
2 eggs, beaten
1 teaspoon vanilla
1½ cups flaked coconut
1 cup toffee baking pieces

1. Preheat oven to 350°F. Line cookie sheets with parchment paper.

2. Combine flour, baking powder and salt in small bowl; set aside. Place 1 cup chocolate chips and butter in large microwavable bowl. Microwave at HIGH 1 minute; stir. Microwave at additional 30-second intervals or until mixture is melted and smooth; stir well.

3. Add brown sugar, eggs and vanilla to chocolate mixture; beat until well blended. Add flour mixture; beat until blended. Stir in coconut, toffee pieces and remaining 1 cup chocolate chips.

4. Drop dough by heaping ⅓ cupfuls about 3 inches apart onto prepared cookie sheets. Flatten with rubber spatula into 3½-inch circles. Bake 15 to 17 minutes or until edges are just firm to the touch. Cool on cookie sheets 2 minutes; slide parchment paper and cookies onto wire rack. Cool completely. *Makes 12 (5-inch) cookies*

Chocolate-Coconut-Toffee Delights

Lemon Pecan Cookies

**1 Butter Flavor CRISCO® Stick or 1 cup Butter Flavor CRISCO®
  all-vegetable shortening**
1½ cups granulated sugar
  2 eggs
  3 tablespoons fresh lemon juice
  3 cups all-purpose flour
  2 teaspoons baking powder
  ¼ teaspoon salt
  1 cup chopped pecans

1. Heat oven to 350°F. Place wire rack on countertop for cooling cookies.

2. Combine 1 cup shortening and sugar in large bowl. Beat at medium speed of electric mixer until well blended. Beat in eggs and lemon juice until well blended.

3. Combine flour, baking powder and salt in medium bowl. Add to creamed mixture; mix well. Stir in nuts. Spray cookie sheets lightly with CRISCO® No-Stick Cooking Spray. Drop dough by teaspoonfuls about 2 inches apart onto prepared cookie sheets. Bake at 350°F for 10 to 12 minutes or until lightly browned. Cool on cookie sheets 4 minutes; transfer to cooling rack to cool completely.

Makes about 6 dozen cookies

tip

A lemon will yield more juice if it is at room temperature. To quickly warm a cold lemon, first microwave it at HIGH for 20 to 30 seconds. Then roll it around on the counter under the palm of your hand before cutting it in half. This releases juice from the small sacs of the lemon. A reamer or juicer can then be used to extract the juice.

Lemon Pecan Cookies

Prized Peanut Butter Crunch Cookies

**1 Butter Flavor CRISCO® Stick or 1 cup Butter Flavor CRISCO®
    all-vegetable shortening**
2 cups firmly packed brown sugar
1 cup JIF® Extra Crunchy Peanut Butter
4 egg whites, lightly beaten
1 teaspoon vanilla
2 cups all-purpose flour
1 teaspoon baking soda
½ teaspoon baking powder
2 cups crisp rice cereal
1½ cups chopped peanuts
1 cup quick oats (not instant or old-fashioned)
1 cup flake coconut

1. Heat oven to 350°F. Place sheets of foil on countertop for cooling cookies.

2. Combine 1 cup shortening, sugar and peanut butter in large bowl. Beat at medium speed of electric mixer until blended. Beat in egg whites and vanilla.

3. Combine flour, baking soda and baking powder. Mix into creamed mixture at low speed until just blended. Stir in, one at a time, rice cereal, nuts, oats and coconut with spoon.

4. Drop rounded measuring tablespoonfuls of dough 2 inches apart onto ungreased baking sheet.

5. Bake at 350°F, one baking sheet at a time, for 8 to 10 minutes, or until set. *Do not overbake.* Remove cookies to foil to cool completely.

Makes about 4 dozen cookies

Prized Peanut Butter Crunch Cookies

fabulous pies & tarts

Chocolate Fudge Pie

Crust
    1 unbaked Classic CRISCO® Single Crust (page 276)

Filling
    ¼ CRISCO® Stick or ¼ cup CRISCO® all-vegetable shortening
    1 bar (4 ounces) sweet baking chocolate
    1 can (14 ounces) sweetened condensed milk
    ½ cup all-purpose flour
    2 eggs, beaten
    1 teaspoon vanilla
    ¼ teaspoon salt
    1 cup flake coconut
    1 cup chopped pecans

Garnish
    Unsweetened whipped cream or ice cream

1. For crust, prepare as directed. Do not bake. Heat oven to 350°F. Place wire rack on countertop for cooling pie.

2. For filling, melt ¼ cup shortening and chocolate in heavy saucepan over low heat. Remove from heat. Stir in sweetened condensed milk, flour, eggs, vanilla and salt; mix well. Stir in coconut and nuts. Pour into unbaked pie crust.

3. Bake at 350°F for 40 minutes or until toothpick inserted into center comes out clean. Cool completely on wire rack.

4. Serve with unsweetened whipped cream or ice cream, if desired. Refrigerate leftover pie.   *Makes 1 (9-inch) pie (8 servings)*

continued on page 276

Chocolate Fudge Pie

Chocolate Fudge Pie, continued

Classic Crisco® Single Crust

1⅓ cups all-purpose flour
½ teaspoon salt
½ CRISCO® Stick or ½ cup CRISCO® all-vegetable shortening
3 tablespoons cold water

1. Spoon flour into measuring cup and level. Combine flour and salt in medium bowl.

2. Cut in ½ cup shortening using pastry blender or 2 knives until all flour is blended to form pea-size chunks.

3. Sprinkle with water, 1 tablespoon at a time. Toss lightly with fork until dough forms a ball.

4. Press dough between hands to form 5- to 6-inch "pancake." Flour rolling surface and rolling pin lightly. Roll dough into circle. Trim circle 1 inch larger than upside-down pie plate. Carefully remove trimmed dough. Set aside to reroll and use for pastry cutout garnish, if desired.

5. Fold dough into quarters. Unfold and press into pie plate. Fold edge under. Flute.

6. **For recipes using a baked pie crust,** heat oven to 425°F. Prick bottom and side thoroughly with fork (50 times) to prevent shrinkage. Bake at 425°F for 10 to 15 minutes or until lightly browned.

7. **For recipes using an unbaked pie crust,** follow directions given for that recipe.   *Makes 1 (9-inch) single crust*

Strawberry Rhubarb Pie

Pastry for double-crust 9-inch pie
4 cups sliced (1-inch pieces) fresh rhubarb
3 cups sliced fresh strawberries
1½ cups sugar
½ cup cornstarch
2 tablespoons quick-cooking tapioca
1 tablespoon grated lemon peel
¼ teaspoon ground allspice
1 egg, lightly beaten

1. Preheat oven to 425°F. Roll out half the pastry; place in 9-inch pie plate. Trim pastry; flute edges, sealing to edge of pie plate. Set aside.

2. Place fruit in large bowl. Combine sugar, cornstarch, tapioca, lemon peel and allspice in medium bowl; mix well. Sprinkle sugar mixture over fruit; toss to coat well. Fill pie shell evenly with fruit. (Do not mound in center.)

3. Roll out remaining pastry to 10-inch circle. Cut into ½-inch-wide strips. Arrange in lattice design over fruit. Brush egg over pastry.

4. Bake 50 minutes or until filling is thick and bubbly. Cool on wire rack. Serve warm or at room temperature. *Makes 8 servings*

tip

Rhubarb is technically a vegetable, but it is used as a fruit. The long, thick, pink or red celerylike stalks are the only edible portion of the plant. The leaves and roots should never be eaten; they contain oxalic acid and are toxic. Store rhubarb in the refrigerator in a plastic bag. It will keep for about three to five days. Cleaned and dried rhubarb stalks can be cut into 1-inch pieces and frozen in a plastic freezer bag for up to nine months.

Deep-Dish Peach Custard Pie

1 *unbaked* 9-inch (4-cup volume) deep-dish pie shell
3½ cups (about 7 medium) peeled, pitted and sliced peaches
1 can (14 ounces) NESTLÉ® CARNATION® Sweetened Condensed Milk
2 eggs
¼ cup butter or margarine, melted
1 to 3 teaspoons lemon juice
½ teaspoon ground cinnamon
   Dash ground nutmeg
   Streusel Topping (recipe follows)

PREHEAT oven to 425°F.

ARRANGE peaches in pie shell. Combine sweetened condensed milk, eggs, butter, lemon juice, cinnamon and nutmeg in large mixer bowl; beat until smooth. Pour over peaches.

BAKE for 10 minutes. Sprinkle with Streusel Topping. Reduce oven temperature to 350°F.; bake for additional 55 to 60 minutes or until knife inserted near center comes out clean. Cool on wire rack.   *Makes 8 servings*

Streusel Topping: COMBINE ⅓ cup all-purpose flour, ⅓ cup packed brown sugar and ⅓ cup chopped walnuts in medium bowl. Cut in 2 tablespoons butter or margarine with pastry blender or two knives until mixture resembles coarse crumbs.

Egg Custard Pie

1 cup sugar
1 cup evaporated milk
2 eggs
1 teaspoon vanilla
1 (9-inch) unbaked pie shell
½ teaspoon butter

Preheat oven to 325°F. Combine sugar, evaporated milk, eggs and vanilla in medium saucepan. Heat over high heat 2 to 3 minutes, stirring constantly. Pour into pie shell. Dot with butter. Bake 40 minutes or until knife inserted into center comes out clean.

Makes 8 servings

Deep-Dish Peach Custard Pie

Rustic Apple Tart with Crème Chantilly

Rustic Tart Dough (page 282)
2 pounds Golden Delicious apples, peeled, cored and cut into
   ½-inch wedges
2 tablespoons lemon juice
½ cup plus 2 tablespoons sugar, divided
½ cup raisins
3 tablespoons plus 1½ teaspoons apple brandy,* divided
1 teaspoon ground cinnamon
3 tablespoons unsalted butter, cut into 6 to 8 pieces
1 cup apricot jam
   Crème Chantilly (page 282)

*Any brandy or cognac can be substituted.

1. Prepare Rustic Tart Dough.

2. Preheat oven to 400°F. Toss apples with lemon juice in large bowl. Add ½ cup sugar, raisins, 2 tablespoons brandy and cinnamon. Toss gently to mix; set aside.

3. Cut piece of parchment paper to fit 15×10-inch jelly-roll pan. Place parchment on counter; sprinkle with flour. Place dough on parchment; sprinkle with flour. Roll dough into 18×16-inch oval about ¼ inch thick. Transfer parchment and dough to baking sheet.

4. Place apple mixture onto center of dough, spreading to within 2 inches of edges. Dot apple mixture with butter. Fold edge of dough up and over filling, overlapping as necessary. Press gently to seal seams. (Center of tart will remain open.) Sprinkle edge of dough with remaining 2 tablespoons sugar.

5. Bake 50 to 55 minutes or until crust is golden brown and apples are tender. Cool slightly.

6. Meanwhile, strain jam through sieve into small saucepan. Stir over low heat until jam is smooth. Stir in remaining 1½ teaspoons brandy. Brush warm tart with jam mixture. Serve with Crème Chantilly. *Makes 8 servings*

continued on page 282

Rustic Apple Tart with Crème Chantilly

Rustic Apple Tart with Crème Chantilly, continued

Rustic Tart Dough

2 cups all-purpose flour
1 teaspoon sugar
1 teaspoon grated lemon peel
½ teaspoon salt
½ teaspoon ground cinnamon
½ cup shortening, chilled
½ cup (1 stick) unsalted cold butter, cut into ¼-inch dice
⅓ cup ice water

1. Place flour, sugar, lemon peel, salt and cinnamon in food processor; process until blended.

2. Add shortening; process using on/off pulsing action until mixture forms pea-sized chunks. Add butter; process using on/off pulsing action until dough resembles coarse crumbs. Add ice water and process just until dough begins to come together. Shape dough into 6-inch disc; wrap in plastic wrap. Refrigerate at least 1 hour or overnight.

Crème Chantilly

1 cup whipping cream
1 tablespoon apple brandy
½ to 1 tablespoon sugar

1. Beat cream in chilled medium bowl with chilled beaters until soft peaks form. Add brandy and sugar to taste; beat until stiff peaks form. *Do not overbeat.*

2. Refrigerate until ready to serve.

Spiced Pear Tart

30 gingersnap cookies
½ cup chopped pecans
⅓ cup butter, melted
1 cup sour cream
¾ cup half-and-half
1 package (4-serving size) instant vanilla pudding mix
2 tablespoons apricot brandy
4 ripe pears*
⅓ cup packed dark brown sugar
¼ teaspoon ground ginger
¼ teaspoon ground cinnamon
⅛ teaspoon ground cloves

Or, substitute 1 (16-ounce) can pear halves, drained and thinly sliced.

1. Preheat oven to 350°F. Combine gingersnaps and pecans in food processor or blender; process until finely crushed. Combine crumb mixture and butter in medium bowl. Press firmly onto bottom and up side of 10-inch quiche dish or 9-inch pie plate. Bake 7 minutes; cool completely on wire rack.

2. Combine sour cream and half-and-half in large bowl; beat until smooth. Whisk in pudding mix. Add apricot brandy; beat until smooth. Pour into prepared pie crust. Cover; refrigerate several hours or overnight.

3. Just before serving, preheat broiler. Peel pears. Cut into thin slices. Arrange in overlapping circles on top of pudding mixture. Combine brown sugar, ginger, cinnamon and cloves in small bowl. Sprinkle evenly over pears. Broil 4 to 6 minutes or until sugar is melted and bubbly. (Watch carefully so sugar does not burn.) Serve immediately. *Makes 6 to 8 servings*

Pineapple Sweet Potato Pie

2 cups mashed cooked sweet potatoes
⅔ cup firmly packed brown sugar
¼ cup half-and-half
1 egg, beaten
2 tablespoons butter or margarine, melted
1 teaspoon vanilla extract, divided
½ teaspoon ground cinnamon
¼ teaspoon ground nutmeg
¼ teaspoon salt
1 (9-inch) pastry shell, unbaked
1 can (15¼ ounces) DEL MONTE® Sliced Pineapple In Its Own Juice, undrained
1 teaspoon cornstarch
1 teaspoon minced candied ginger

1. Combine sweet potatoes, brown sugar, half-and-half, egg, butter, ½ teaspoon vanilla, cinnamon, nutmeg and salt; mix well. Pour into pastry shell.

2. Bake at 425°F, 25 to 30 minutes or until set in center; cool.

3. Drain pineapple, reserving ½ cup juice. Pour reserved juice into small saucepan. Add cornstarch; stir until dissolved. Cook, stirring constantly, until thickened and translucent. Stir in ginger and remaining ½ teaspoon vanilla.

4. Cut pineapple slices in half; arrange pineapple over pie. Spoon juice mixture over pineapple. Garnish, if desired. *Makes 8 servings*

Prep and Cook Time: 1 hour

Pineapple Sweet Potato Pie

White Chocolate Cranberry Tart

1 refrigerated pie crust (half of 15-ounce package)
1 cup sugar
2 eggs
¼ cup (½ stick) butter, melted
2 teaspoons vanilla
½ cup all-purpose flour
1 package (6 ounces) white chocolate, chopped
½ cup chopped macadamia nuts, lightly toasted*
½ cup dried cranberries, coarsely chopped

*Toast chopped macadamia nuts in hot skillet over medium heat about 3 minutes or until fragrant.

1. Preheat oven to 350°F. Place pie crust in 9-inch tart pan with removable bottom or pie pan. (Refrigerate or freeze other crust for another use.)

2. Combine sugar, eggs, butter and vanilla in large bowl; mix well. Stir in flour until well blended. Add white chocolate, nuts and cranberries.

3. Pour filling into unbaked crust. Bake 50 to 55 minutes or until top of tart is crusty and deep golden brown and knife inserted into center comes out clean.

4. Cool completely on wire rack.   *Makes 8 servings*

Serving Suggestion: Top each serving with a dollop of whipped cream flavored with ground cinnamon, a favorite liqueur and grated orange peel.

tip

The marvelous macadamia nut is second to none for its buttery smooth flavor and delectable crunch. It is the world's most expensive nut and considered by many to also be the world's finest. Native to Australia, the macadamia tree was named after the man who cultivated it, chemist John MacAdam. It was brought to Hawaii in the late nineteenth century and has since become the state's third largest crop.

White Chocolate Cranberry Tart

Nectarine Pecan Tart

Pecan Crust
>**1 cup vanilla wafer crumbs**
>**½ cup pecan pieces**
>**2 tablespoons sugar**
>**3 tablespoons unsalted butter, melted**

Cream Cheese Filling
>**1 package (8 ounces) plus 1 package (3 ounces) cream cheese, softened**
>**3 tablespoons sugar**
>**2 tablespoons orange juice**
>**½ teaspoon vanilla**

Fruit Topping
>**2 ripe nectarines**
>**¼ cup apricot jelly**

1. For crust, preheat oven to 350°F. Place wafer crumbs, pecans and sugar in food processor; process until coarse crumbs form. Transfer to small bowl; stir in butter. Press crumb mixture onto bottom and partially up side of 8-inch springform pan.

2. Bake 15 minutes or until lightly browned. Cool completely on wire rack.

3. For filling, beat cream cheese, sugar, juice and vanilla in medium bowl with electric mixer at low speed until blended. Increase speed to high; beat 2 minutes or until fluffy.

4. Spread filling evenly in cooled crust. Cover; refrigerate 3 hours or until set.

5. For topping, 30 minutes before serving, cut nectarines into thin slices. Arrange nectarine slices over filling. Melt jelly in small saucepan, whisking constantly, over low heat. Cool 1 minute. Drizzle jelly over nectarines. Refrigerate, uncovered, 20 minutes or until set.   *Makes 6 servings*

Note: For best results, serve tart same day as assembled.

Nectarine Pecan Tart

Double Blueberry Cheese Pie

Crust
   1 unbaked Classic CRISCO® Single Crust (page 276)

Filling
   2 packages (8 ounces each) cream cheese, softened
   1 cup granulated sugar
   2 tablespoons all-purpose flour
   2 eggs
   2 teaspoons vanilla
   ½ cup whipping cream
   2 cups fresh blueberries

Topping
   2 cups whipping cream
   2 tablespoons confectioners' sugar
   1 teaspoon vanilla
   1 cup fresh blueberries

1. For crust, prepare as directed using 9- or 9½-inch deep-dish pie plate. Do not bake. Heat oven to 350°F.

2. For filling, place cream cheese and granulated sugar in food processor bowl. Process, using steel blade, until smooth. Add flour, eggs, 2 teaspoons vanilla and ½ cup whipping cream through feed tube while processor is running. Process until blended. Add 2 cups blueberries. Pulse (quick on and off) twice. Pour into unbaked pie crust.

3. Bake at 350°F for 45 minutes. *Do not overbake.* Turn off oven. Allow pie to remain in oven with door ajar for 1 hour. Cool to room temperature. Refrigerate 6 hours or overnight.

4. For topping, beat 2 cups whipping cream in large bowl at high speed of electric mixer until stiff peaks form. Beat in confectioners' sugar and 1 teaspoon vanilla. Spread over top of pie. Garnish with 1 cup blueberries. Serve immediately. Refrigerate leftover pie.   *Makes 1 (9- or 9½-inch) deep-dish pie (8 servings)*

Double Blueberry Cheese Pie

Fruit Tart

⅓ cup **FLEISCHMANN'S® Original Margarine**
1¼ cups **all-purpose flour**
4 to 5 tablespoons **ice water**
1 cup **EGG BEATERS®**
⅓ cup **sugar**
1 teaspoon **vanilla extract**
1¼ cups **skim milk, scalded**
1 cup **sliced fresh fruit**

In medium bowl, cut margarine into flour until mixture resembles coarse crumbs. Add water, 1 tablespoon at a time, tossing until moistened. Shape into a ball. On floured surface, roll dough into 11-inch circle, about ⅛ inch thick. Place in 9-inch pie plate, making a ½-inch-high fluted edge; set aside.

In medium bowl, combine Egg Beaters®, sugar and vanilla; gradually stir in milk. Pour into prepared crust. Bake at 350°F for 45 to 50 minutes or until set. Cool completely on wire rack. Cover; chill until firm, about 2 hours. To serve, top with fruit.

Makes 10 servings

Prep Time: 30 minutes
Bake Time: 45 minutes

Southern Peanut Pie

3 eggs
1½ cups **dark corn syrup**
½ cup **granulated sugar**
¼ cup **butter, melted**
½ teaspoon **vanilla extract**
¼ teaspoon **salt**
1½ cups **chopped roasted peanuts**
9-inch **unbaked deep-dish pastry shell**

Beat eggs until foamy. Add corn syrup, sugar, butter, vanilla and salt; continue to beat until thoroughly blended. Stir in peanuts. Pour into unbaked pastry shell. Bake in preheated 375°F oven 50 to 55 minutes. Serve warm or cold. Garnish with whipped cream or ice cream, if desired.

Makes 6 servings

Favorite recipe from **Texas Peanut Producers Board**

Fruit Tart

Traditional Pumpkin Pie

1 (15-ounce) can pumpkin
1 (14-ounce) can EAGLE BRAND® Sweetened Condensed Milk
(NOT evaporated milk)
2 eggs
1 teaspoon ground cinnamon
½ teaspoon salt
½ teaspoon ground ginger
½ teaspoon ground nutmeg
1 (9-inch) unbaked pastry shell
Favorite Topping (recipes follow), if desired

1. Preheat oven to 425°F. In large mixing bowl, combine all ingredients except pastry shell and Favorite Topping; mix well.

2. Pour into pastry shell. Bake 15 minutes.

3. Reduce oven temperature to 350°F. Continue baking 35 to 40 minutes, or as directed with one Favorite Topping, if desired, or until knife inserted 1 inch from edge comes out clean. Cool. Garnish as desired. Store covered in refrigerator.

Makes one 9-inch pie

Sour Cream Topping: In medium mixing bowl, combine 1½ cups sour cream, 2 tablespoons sugar and 1 teaspoon vanilla extract. After pie has baked 30 minutes at 350°F, spread evenly over top; bake 10 minutes.

Chocolate Glaze: In heavy saucepan over low heat, melt ½ cup semi-sweet chocolate chips and 1 teaspoon solid vegetable shortening. Drizzle or spread over top of baked and cooled pie.

Streusel Topping: In medium mixing bowl, combine ½ cup all-purpose flour and ½ cup firmly packed light brown sugar; cut in ¼ cup (½ stick) cold butter or margarine until crumbly. Stir in ¼ cup chopped nuts. After pie has baked 30 minutes at 350°F, sprinkle evenly over top; bake 10 minutes.

Prep Time: 20 minutes
Bake Time: 50 to 55 minutes

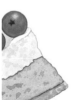

Traditional Pumpkin Pie

Chocolate Strawberry Fruit Tart

1⅓ **cups all-purpose flour**
½ **cup powdered sugar**
¼ **cup HERSHEY'S Cocoa or HERSHEY'S Dutch Processed Cocoa**
¾ **cup (1½ sticks) butter or margarine, softened**
   Strawberry Vanilla Filling (page 298)
½ **cup HERSHEY'S Semi-Sweet Chocolate Chips**
 1 **tablespoon shortening (do *not* use butter, margarine, spread or oil)**
   Glazed Fruit Topping (page 298)
   Fresh fruit, sliced

1. Heat oven to 325°F. Grease and flour 12-inch pizza pan.

2. Stir together flour, powdered sugar and cocoa in medium bowl. With pastry blender, cut in butter until mixture holds together; press into prepared pan.

3. Bake 10 to 15 minutes or until crust is set. Cool completely.

4. Prepare Strawberry Filling; spread over crust to within 1 inch of edge; refrigerate until filling is firm.

5. Place chocolate chips and shortening in small microwave-safe bowl. Microwave at HIGH (100% power) 30 seconds; stir. If necessary, microwave at HIGH an additional 15 seconds at a time, stirring after each heating, just until chips are melted when stirred. Spoon chocolate into disposable pastry bag or corner of heavy duty plastic bag; cut off small piece at corner. Squeeze chocolate onto outer edge of filling in decorative design; refrigerate until chocolate is firm.

6. Prepare Glazed Fruit Topping. Arrange fresh fruit over filling; carefully brush prepared topping over fruit. Refrigerate until ready to serve. Cover; refrigerate leftover tart.
Makes 12 servings

continued on page 298

Chocolate Strawberry Fruit Tart

Chocolate Strawberry Fruit Tart, continued

Strawberry Vanilla Filling

**1⅔ cups (10-ounce package) or 2 cups (12-ounce package)
HERSHEY¡S Premier White Chips
¼ cup evaporated milk
1 package (8 ounces) cream cheese, softened
1 teaspoon strawberry extract
2 drops red food color**

1. Place white chips and evaporated milk in medium microwave-safe bowl. Microwave at HIGH (100% power) 1 minute; stir. If necessary, microwave at HIGH an additional 15 seconds at a time, stirring after each heating, just until chips are melted when stirred.

2. Beat in cream cheese, strawberry extract and red food color.

Glazed Fruit Topping

**¼ teaspoon unflavored gelatin
1 teaspoon cold water
1½ teaspoons cornstarch *or* arrowroot
¼ cup apricot nectar *or* orange juice
2 tablespoons sugar
½ teaspoon lemon juice**

1. Sprinkle gelatin over water in small cup; let stand 2 minutes to soften.

2. Stir together cornstarch, apricot nectar, sugar and lemon juice in small saucepan. Cook over medium heat, stirring constantly, until mixture is thickened. Remove from heat; immediately stir in gelatin until smooth. Cool slightly.

tip

When heated, gelatin mixtures should never be brought to a boil or the ability of the gelatin to set will be destroyed.

Cranberry Peach Tart with Almonds

Crust
    Prepared frozen or refrigerated pastry for one-crust 9-inch pie

Filling
    3 cups frozen sliced peaches (20-ounce package), thawed
    1 cup fresh or frozen cranberries, thawed
    ½ cup DOMINO® Granulated Sugar
    ¼ cup all purpose flour
    ½ teaspoon nutmeg
    ¼ teaspoon salt

Topping
    ⅔ cup all-purpose flour
    ½ cup firmly packed DOMINO® Light Brown Sugar
    ½ teaspoon cinnamon
    ⅓ cup butter or margarine, softened
    ½ cup slivered almonds

Heat oven to 425°F. Line 9-inch tart pan or pie pan with pastry; trim edges until pastry is even with top edge of pan. Prick bottom of pastry with fork. Bake 10 minutes. Remove from oven. Reduce oven temperature to 375°F.

Combine filling ingredients in large bowl, tossing gently until well mixed. Spread evenly in partially-baked crust.

Combine ⅔ cup flour, brown sugar and cinnamon in small bowl. Cut in butter; stir in almonds. Sprinkle evenly over filling. Bake 40 to 50 minutes or until filling is bubbly. Cover tart loosely with foil during last 15 to 20 minutes of baking to prevent overbrowning.
Makes 6 to 8 servings

Prep Time: 30 minutes
Bake Time: 1 hour

Variation: For Blueberry Peach Tart with Almonds, substitute fresh or frozen blueberries, thawed, for the cranberries. Proceed as directed.

Nestlé® Toll House® Chocolate Chip Pie

    2 eggs
    ½ cup all-purpose flour
    ½ cup granulated sugar
    ½ cup packed brown sugar
    ¾ cup (1½ sticks) butter, softened
    1 cup (6 ounces) NESTLÉ® TOLL HOUSE® Semi-Sweet Chocolate Morsels
    1 cup chopped nuts
    1 *unbaked* 9-inch (4-cup volume) deep-dish pie shell*
      Sweetened whipped cream or ice cream (optional)

If using frozen pie shell, use deep-dish style, thawed completely. Bake on baking sheet; increase baking time slightly.

PREHEAT oven to 325°F.

BEAT eggs in large mixer bowl on high speed until foamy. Beat in flour, granulated sugar and brown sugar. Beat in butter. Stir in morsels and nuts. Spoon into pie shell.

BAKE for 55 to 60 minutes or until knife inserted halfway between outside edge and center comes out clean. Cool on wire rack. Serve warm with whipped cream.

Makes 8 servings

Peanut Crumb Apple Pie

    1 cup all-purpose flour
    ½ cup SMUCKER'S® Creamy Natural Peanut Butter or JIF® Creamy
      Peanut Butter
    ½ cup firmly packed light brown sugar
    ¼ cup butter or margarine, softened
    ¼ teaspoon salt
    1 can (30-ounce) apple pie filling
    1 (9-inch) unbaked pie shell

Blend flour, peanut butter, brown sugar, butter and salt until mixture is crumbly. Spoon apple pie filling into unbaked crust; sprinkle peanut butter mixture over pie filling.

Bake at 400°F for 30 to 35 minutes or until filling is hot and pastry is browned.

Makes 6 to 8 servings

Nestlé® Toll House® Chocolate Chip Pie

Cider Apple Pie in Cheddar Crust

Crust
   2 cups sifted all-purpose flour
   1 cup shredded Cheddar cheese
   ½ teaspoon salt
   ⅔ **CRISCO**® Stick or ⅔ cup **CRISCO**® all-vegetable shortening
   5 to 6 tablespoons ice water

Filling
   6 cups sliced peeled apples (about 2 pounds or 6 medium)
   1 cup apple cider
   ⅔ cup granulated sugar
   2 tablespoons cornstarch
   2 tablespoons water
   ½ teaspoon ground cinnamon
   1 tablespoon butter or margarine

Glaze
   1 egg yolk
   1 tablespoon water

1. Heat oven to 400°F. For crust, place flour, cheese and salt in food processor bowl. Add shortening. Process 15 seconds. Sprinkle water through feed tube, 1 tablespoon at a time, until dough just forms (process time not to exceed 20 seconds). Shape into ball. Divide dough in half. Press between hands to form two 5- to 6-inch "pancakes." Roll and press bottom crust into 9-inch pie plate.

2. For filling, combine apples, apple cider and sugar in large saucepan. Cook and stir on medium-high heat until mixture comes to a boil. Reduce heat to low; simmer 5 minutes. Combine cornstarch, water and cinnamon; stir into apples. Cook and stir until mixture comes to a boil. Remove from heat. Stir in butter. Spoon into unbaked pie crust. Moisten pastry edge with water.

3. Roll top crust. Lift onto filled pie. Trim ½ inch beyond edge of pie plate. Fold top edge under bottom crust. Flute. Cut slits or design in top crust to allow steam to escape.

4. For glaze, beat egg yolk with fork. Stir in water. Brush over top. Bake at 400°F for 35 to 40 minutes or until filling in center is bubbly and crust is golden brown. Cover edge with foil, if necessary, to prevent overbrowning. *Do not overbake.* Cool to room temperature before serving.   *Makes 1 (9-inch) pie (8 servings)*

Note: Golden Delicious, Granny Smith and Jonathan apples are all suitable for pie baking.

Cider Apple Pie in Cheddar Crust

Best Cherry Pie

Crust
   1 unbaked Classic CRISCO® Double Crust (page 306)

Filling
   ¾ cup sugar
   3 tablespoons flour
   ⅛ teaspoon salt
   ¼ cup cherry juice
   Few drops red food coloring (optional)
   2 cans (16 ounces each) drained red sour pitted cherries
   1 tablespoon butter or margarine
   ½ teaspoon almond extract (optional)

Glaze
   1 egg
   ¼ cup half-and-half

1. For crust, prepare as directed. Do not bake. Heat oven to 400°F.

2. For filling, combine sugar, flour and salt in medium saucepan. Add cherry juice and red food coloring, if desired; stir until blended. Add cherries. Cook and stir over medium heat until mixture comes to a boil; boil 1 minute. Remove from heat; stir in butter and almond extract, if desired.

3. Pour filling into unbaked pie crust. Roll out top crust. Using 1½-inch star cutter, cut 3 stars in center of crust. Place top crust over filling; trim and seal. Roll out leftover scraps to ⅛-inch thickness; cut into star garnishes. Place on crust as desired.

4. For glaze, beat egg yolk with fork. Stir in half-and-half. Brush over top. Bake at 400°F for about 30 minutes or until filling in center is bubbly and crust is golden brown. Cover edge with foil, if necessary, to prevent overbrowning. *Do not overbake.*
Makes one 9-inch pie

continued on page 306

Best Cherry Pie

Best Cherry Pie, continued

Classic Crisco® Double Crust

2 cups all-purpose flour
1 teaspoon salt
¾ CRISCO® Stick or ¾ cup CRISCO® all-vegetable shortening
5 tablespoons cold water (or more as needed)

1. Spoon flour into measuring cup and level. Combine flour and salt in medium bowl.

2. Cut in ¾ cup shortening using pastry blender or 2 knives until all flour is blended to form pea-size chunks.

3. Sprinkle with water, 1 tablespoon at a time. Toss lightly with fork until dough forms a ball. Divide dough in half.

4. Press dough between hands to form two 5- to 6-inch "pancakes." Flour rolling surface and rolling pin lightly. Roll both halves of dough into circles. Trim one circle of dough 1 inch larger than upside-down pie plate. Carefully remove trimmed dough. Set aside to reroll and use for pastry cutout garnish, if desired.

5. Fold dough into quarters. Unfold and press into pie plate. Trim edge even with plate. Add desired filling to unbaked crust. Moisten pastry edge with water. Lift top crust onto filled pie. Trim ½ inch beyond edge of pie plate. Fold top edge under bottom crust. Flute. Cut slits in top crust to allow steam to escape. Follow baking directions given for that recipe.   *Makes 1 (9-inch) double crust*

Farmhouse Lemon Meringue Pie

1 frozen pie crust
4 eggs, at room temperature
3 tablespoons lemon juice
2 tablespoons butter or margarine, melted
2 teaspoons grated lemon peel
3 drops yellow food coloring (optional)
⅔ cup sugar, divided
1 cup cold water
¼ cup cornstarch
⅛ teaspoon salt
¼ teaspoon vanilla

1. Preheat oven to 425°F. Bake pie crust according to package directions. Cool on wire rack.

2. Separate eggs, discarding 2 egg yolks; set aside. Mix lemon juice, butter, lemon peel and food coloring, if desired, in small bowl; set aside.

3. Reserve 2 tablespoons sugar. Combine water, remaining sugar, cornstarch and salt in medium saucepan; whisk until smooth. Heat over medium-high heat, whisking constantly, until mixture begins to boil. Reduce heat to medium. Continue to boil 1 minute, stirring constantly; remove from heat.

4. Stir ¼ cup boiling sugar mixture into egg yolks; whisk constantly until completely blended. Slowly whisk egg yolk mixture back into boiling sugar mixture. Cook over medium heat 3 minutes, whisking constantly. Remove from heat; stir in lemon juice mixture until well blended. Pour into baked pie crust.

5. Beat egg whites in large bowl with electric mixer at high speed until soft peaks form. Gradually beat in reserved 2 tablespoons sugar and vanilla; beat until stiff peaks form. Spread meringue over pie filling with rubber spatula, making sure meringue completely covers filling and touches edge of pie crust.

6. Bake 15 minutes. Remove from oven; cool completely on wire rack. Cover with plastic wrap; refrigerate 8 hours or overnight until pie is set and thoroughly chilled. Garnish as desired. *Makes 8 servings*

Wisconsin Ricotta Tart with Kiwi and Raspberry Sauce

⅓ cup all-purpose flour
⅓ cup packed brown sugar
3 tablespoons butter
1 cup flaked coconut
½ cup chopped pecans or macadamia nuts
2 cups (16 ounces) Wisconsin Ricotta cheese
½ cup powdered sugar
1 teaspoon grated lime peel
1 teaspoon vanilla
1 package (10 ounces) frozen raspberries, thawed
1 kiwifruit

Preheat oven to 350°F. Combine flour and brown sugar; cut in butter until mixture resembles coarse crumbs. Stir in coconut and nuts. Press into 10-inch tart pan or pie plate. Bake crust 15 minutes. Remove from oven and cool.

Combine cheese, powdered sugar, lime peel and vanilla in food processor or blender; process until smooth. Spoon mixture into prepared crust. Refrigerate 1 hour. Before serving, place raspberries in food processor or blender; process until sauce forms. Cut kiwi into slices and arrange in circle on top of tart.* Drizzle tart with ½ of the raspberry sauce. Serve with remaining sauce. *Makes 8 to 10 servings*

*Recipe can be prepared to this point and refrigerated until ready to serve.

Favorite recipe from **Wisconsin Milk Marketing Board**

Wisconsin Ricotta Tart with Kiwi and Raspberry Sauce

Rice Pudding Tarts

1 cup cooked rice
1 cup low-fat milk
⅓ cup sugar
¼ cup raisins
⅛ teaspoon salt
2 eggs, beaten
¾ cup heavy cream
½ teaspoon vanilla extract
¼ teaspoon almond extract
6 frozen tartlet pastry shells, partially baked and cooled
⅛ teaspoon ground nutmeg for garnish
Fresh berries for garnish
Fresh mint for garnish

Combine rice, milk, sugar, raisins and salt in medium saucepan. Cook over medium-low heat 30 to 35 minutes or until thick and creamy, stirring frequently. Remove from heat; add ¼ of rice mixture to eggs. Return egg mixture to saucepan; stir in cream and extracts. Spoon equally into pastry shells; sprinkle with nutmeg. Place tarts on baking sheet. Bake at 350°F 20 to 30 minutes or until pudding is set. Cool on wire rack 1 hour. Unmold tarts and garnish with berries and mint. Serve at room temperature. Refrigerate remaining tarts. *Makes 6 servings*

*Favorite recipe from **USA Rice***

Acknowledgments

The publisher would like to thank the companies and organizations listed below for the use of their recipes and photographs in this publication.

Arm & Hammer Division, Church & Dwight Co., Inc.

Cherry Marketing Institute

Crisco is a registered trademark of The J.M. Smucker Company

Del Monte Corporation

Dole Food Company, Inc.

Domino® Foods, Inc.

Duncan Hines® and Moist Deluxe® are registered trademarks of Pinnacle Foods Corp.

Eagle Brand® Sweetened Condensed Milk

Egg Beaters®

Fleischmann's® Yeast

Grandma's® is a registered trademark of Mott's, LLP

Hershey Foods Corporation

© Mars, Incorporated 2005

McIlhenny Company (TABASCO® brand Pepper Sauce)

Mott's® is a registered trademark of Mott's, LLP

National Honey Board

Nestlé USA

North Dakota Wheat Commission

The Quaker® Oatmeal Kitchens

Reckitt Benckiser Inc.

RED STAR® Yeast, a product of Lasaffre Yeast Corporation

Sargento® Foods Inc.

Smucker's® trademark of The J.M. Smucker Company

The Sugar Association, Inc.

Sun•Maid® Growers of California

Texas Peanut Producers Board

Unilever Foods North America

Washington Apple Commission

Wisconsin Milk Marketing Board

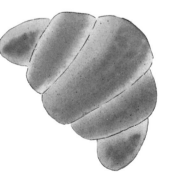

Index

METRIC CONVERSION CHART

VOLUME MEASUREMENTS (dry)

$1/8$ teaspoon = 0.5 mL
$1/4$ teaspoon = 1 mL
$1/2$ teaspoon = 2 mL
$3/4$ teaspoon = 4 mL
1 teaspoon = 5 mL
1 tablespoon = 15 mL
2 tablespoons = 30 mL
$1/4$ cup = 60 mL
$1/3$ cup = 75 mL
$1/2$ cup = 125 mL
$2/3$ cup = 150 mL
$3/4$ cup = 175 mL
1 cup = 250 mL
2 cups = 1 pint = 500 mL
3 cups = 750 mL
4 cups = 1 quart = 1 L

VOLUME MEASUREMENTS (fluid)

1 fluid ounce (2 tablespoons) = 30 mL
4 fluid ounces ($1/2$ cup) = 125 mL
8 fluid ounces (1 cup) = 250 mL
12 fluid ounces ($1 1/2$ cups) = 375 mL
16 fluid ounces (2 cups) = 500 mL

WEIGHTS (mass)

$1/2$ ounce = 15 g
1 ounce = 30 g
3 ounces = 90 g
4 ounces = 120 g
8 ounces = 225 g
10 ounces = 285 g
12 ounces = 360 g
16 ounces = 1 pound = 450 g

DIMENSIONS

$1/16$ inch = 2 mm
$1/8$ inch = 3 mm
$1/4$ inch = 6 mm
$1/2$ inch = 1.5 cm
$3/4$ inch = 2 cm
1 inch = 2.5 cm

OVEN TEMPERATURES

250°F = 120°C
275°F = 140°C
300°F = 150°C
325°F = 160°C
350°F = 180°C
375°F = 190°C
400°F = 200°C
425°F = 220°C
450°F = 230°C

BAKING PAN SIZES

Utensil	Size in Inches/Quarts	Metric Volume	Size in Centimeters
Baking or Cake Pan (square or rectangular)	$8 \times 8 \times 2$	2 L	$20 \times 20 \times 5$
	$9 \times 9 \times 2$	2.5 L	$23 \times 23 \times 5$
	$12 \times 8 \times 2$	3 L	$30 \times 20 \times 5$
	$13 \times 9 \times 2$	3.5 L	$33 \times 23 \times 5$
Loaf Pan	$8 \times 4 \times 3$	1.5 L	$20 \times 10 \times 7$
	$9 \times 5 \times 3$	2 L	$23 \times 13 \times 7$
Round Layer Cake Pan	$8 \times 1 1/2$	1.2 L	20×4
	$9 \times 1 1/2$	1.5 L	23×4
Pie Plate	$8 \times 1 1/4$	750 mL	20×3
	$9 \times 1 1/4$	1 L	23×3
Baking Dish or Casserole	1 quart	1 L	—
	$1 1/2$ quart	1.5 L	—
	2 quart	2 L	—